Fragments of a Future Scroll

Fragments of a Future Scroll

Hasidism for the Aquarian Age

50th Anniversary Edition

Reb Zalman Schachter-Shalomi

Editor's Note by Eden Pearlstein
Foreword by Tirzah Firestone
Introduction by Shaul Magid
Afterword by Jericho Vincent
Postscript by Arthur Kurzweil

Ayin Press

Ayin books are made possible through the generous support of the Orphiflamme Foundation, Anne Germanacos, and Lippman Kanfer Foundation for Living Torah, as well as our grassroots donors and members. We are grateful for their commitment to the transformative power of creative work, and to amplifying a polyphony of voices from within and beyond the Jewish world.

Ayin also gratefully acknowledges the following donors and partners for essential support in bringing this reprint to life: the Yesod Board of Directors (Aaron Claman, Rabbi Tirzah Firestone, David Friedman, Thomas Hast, and Bobbie Zelkind), Arthur and Caren Fried, Larry Schwartz and Shelley Levine, Shari and Maurice Herskowitz-Gluckstadt, Alan J. Bernstein and Carol Bowen, Rabbi Terry Bookman, Mark and Kimberly Russo, Rabbi David Ingber and the Romemu community, and Netanel Miles-Yépez.

Part of Reb Zalman's original introduction appeared as an article in *Sh'ma* 4, no. 74 (May 17, 1974).

An earlier version of the Sabbath Time Chart on page 182 was developed in workshops conducted by Reb Zalman, and was subsequently published in the *Jewish Catalog* by the Jewish Publication Society of America.

Cover design by James Goggin
Cover photograph: Reb Zalman Schachter-Shalomi, circa 1975,
used with permission of the Schachter-Shalomi estate

Typeset in Fedra Serif designed by Peter Bil'ak
with Bahman Eslami, Kristyan Sarkis, Khajag Apelian,
Gayaneh Bagdasaryan, Panagiotis Haratzopoulos & Michal Saha
Released by Netherlands-based foundry Typotheque in 2003

50th Anniversary Edition
First Printing

Ayin Press
Brooklyn, New York
www.ayinpress.org
info@ayinpress.org

Distributed by Publishers Group West, an Ingram brand
Printed in the USA

ISBN: 978-1-961814-32-5 (paperback)
ISBN: 978-1-961814-33-2 (e-book)

Library of Congress Control Number: 2025932225

Ayin Press books may be purchased at a discounted rate by wholesalers, booksellers, book clubs, schools, universities, synagogues, community organizations, and other institutions buying in bulk. For more information, please email *info@ayinpress.org*.

Follow us on social media *@AyinPress*.

With honor and joy we dedicate the reissuing of Reb Zalman's *Fragments of a Future Scroll* to the living memory of our beloved Rebbe and prophetic teacher, and to the generations to come, who will drink from the ancient and ever-renewing wells of wisdom that he opened for us all.

THE YESOD FOUNDATION BOARD OF DIRECTORS
Aaron Claman
Rabbi Tirzah Firestone, PhD
David Friedman
Thomas Hast
Bobbie Zelkind, President

In honor of our ancestors, as a blessing for our families and a gift for our future—we are honored to support the perpetual renewal of Jewish spiritual wisdom, life, and culture.

Arthur and Caren Fried
Larry Schwartz and Shelley Levine
Shari and Maurice Herskowitz-Gluckstadt
Alan J. Bernstein and Carol Bowen
Rabbi Terry Bookman

With deep gratitude, we salute all who have been involved with the Elat Chayyim and Isabella Freedman Jewish Retreat Centers. Over many years, these sacred spaces for immersive experience have served as incubators for Reb Zalman's teachings to manifest and grow.

El Rachamim (G-d of Compassion), *Gomel Hasidim Tovim* (Bestower of Beneficial Kindnesses), may the insights, openings, renewal, and divine flow continue to flourish. *Selah*!

Mark and Kimberly Russo

Dedicated to Reb Zalman Schachter-Shalomi, z"l, whose *Fragments of a Future Scroll* remains a paradigm-shifting work fifty years after its original publication. Meeting Zalman was "a chiropractic adjustment for my soul," and the legacy of that transformation birthed Romemu and continues to reverberate in our community today.

Rabbi David Ingber, with gratitude to the Romemu board, staff, and community

Dedicated to all of Reb Zalman's many students, friends, and collaborators from all walks of life—past, present, and future.

HaNistarim

Fragments of a Future Scroll

Part Three: Kabbalistic Foundations

“I still believe in the future scroll … that will serve to guide us past the current paradigm shift.”

—Reb Zalman, “Dedication,” 1982 edition of *Fragments of a Future Scroll*

Editor's Note

We at Ayin Press are overjoyed to publish the 50th anniversary edition of Reb Zalman Schachter-Shalomi's first book, *Fragments of a Future Scroll: Hasidism for the Aquarian Age*. To bring such a groundbreaking text lost to history back into circulation is a publisher's dream. To collaborate with an intergenerational cast of luminaries to uplift, update, reframe, and renew their rebbe's teachings is a neo-Hasid's highest honor.

In preparing this text for publication, many questions arose. First off, *Fragments* is weird, delightfully so. Second, it was written over fifty years ago. Regarding the first issue, we did our best to preserve Reb Zalman's idiosyncratic voice and approach to constructing these "fragments." We made small edits in particularly obtuse points in the syntax and punctuation of certain sentences when we felt that greater clarity would enhance the reader's reception of the essence of the text. But in the vast majority of the book we let Reb Zalman's playful neologisms and quirky turns of phrase remain, as they are more often than not productively disorienting. Another aspect of the text worth mentioning is that Reb Zalman chose not to cite most of the sources he is weaving and translating throughout the book. The result is a book that is not written to academic standards, but rather is more of a poetic-inspired flow of ancient Jewish thought, timeless mystical wisdom, and contemporary literary expression. We added a small handful of endnotes where we thought it would be helpful for the general reader, but we predominantly chose to honor Reb Zalman's original aesthetic in this respect. The annotated edition of *Fragments* is another project for another time, for another purpose.

Regarding the second issue—that of the datedness of certain passages in the book—after a good deal of reflection and consultation, we took a slightly more active editorial approach. In the spirit of renewal, understood as an epistemological orientation, we edited a small handful of passages that we felt quite simply did not land in 2025, and would have only served to distract readers from the more essential transmissions that Reb Zalman was channeling. In going through our deliberations for this approach, we acknowledged that not only were we not preparing a scholarly annotated edition, we were also not producing a facsimile edition of the original text. We took inspiration from Reb Zalman himself as we noted a similarly small handful of changes made between the original 1975 and 1982 printings of this book. Reb Zalman was nothing if not dynamically responsive and creative in his relation to text, tradition, and truth in the flow of time as a living and evolving reality. We did our best to align with that commitment to the ever-flowering *Eitz Chayim*, the Tree of Life.

I would like to express my deep gratitude to Reb Netanel Miles-Yépez, Reb Zalman's longtime collaborator and literary executor, for the trust he placed in us to bring this project to fruition. His grounded presence and sage counsel throughout this process have been absolutely essential on every level. I would also like to thank Rabbi Tirzah Firestone, Rabbi Shaul Magid, Rav Jericho Vincent, and Arthur Kurzweil for their contributions to introduce and frame this particular book and Reb Zalman's way and work in the world more broadly. All of their supplementary writings help to situate new and unfamiliar readers to this strange and beautiful text and Reb Zalman's paradigm-shifting perspective. Special thanks to Shaul for fielding my myriad questions and clarifying numerous points throughout the text and notes. Gratitude goes out as well to Joanna Steinhardt and Josh Kurtz for their editorial acumen and invaluable support at different levels of assessing and crystallizing the text.

This project has required ample doses of chutzpah and humility from all involved. I pray that in the preparation and presentation of this key text in the history of Jewish renewal we have achieved an appropriate balance of both, and that this book, in all of its deep learning, poetic experimentation, and trickster wisdom, finds its way into the hearts of all those in need of tools and inspiration for navigating and codirecting the flow of creative renewal in their lives and in these times. For they are indeed "a-changin'."

Shift happens. Is happening. Always. That is the way of the world. The question for us is, in every moment: How will we respond? *Ayeka?* Where are you? *Fragments of a Future Scroll* is simultaneously a record of Reb Zalman's real-time thinking-through of that archetypal question in 1975, and a prophetic mirror for our own reflections on the current moment as we seek to give life and limb to the messianic mantra of Jewish futurism: *Olam chesed yibaneh*, "The world will be built with generous loving-kindness." May we all merit to embody this ancient prayer in all of our thoughts, words, actions, and relationships. For the good of One and All. Amen.

Eden Pearlstein

Philadelphia, Pennsylvania
January 2025; Tevet 5785

Foreword

The book you are holding in your hands is a sacred artifact, a bold gambit of reinvention, a dislocation of secret treasures from a charred reality, an illicit smuggling into a new world.

It is also an old friend. By the time it was handed to me as a twenty-something, *Fragments of a Future Scroll* was already tattered, a must-read loan from a new friend. (Admittedly, I never returned it.)

To tell you the truth, I had little understanding of what the book was saying back then, or the prodigious moves its author was making. *Fragments* was written in a poetically disorienting style. Its edges were not smooth. It said both too much and too little. And yet I knew, or could feel, that the book had shifted the ground beneath me in powerful ways that would take years to fully understand.

This eccentric, cookbook-style guide to Kabbalah for the modern seeker was, just as the title suggested, composed of fragments of wisdom torn from an eclectic array of spiritual operating manuals, addressing seekers on their path to *devekut*, a life of God-consciousness. It dared me to revisit the world I had rejected—a rigidly masculine Jewish orthodoxy—first by surfacing the submerged sacredness of the sensual, and then by thrusting me into a vast skyful of strange and numinous teachings from my own birth tradition. Moreover, this short yet dense little book unabashedly insisted that its subtle wisdom belonged to me, and was completely compatible with the world I had embraced: the world of interior spaces.

My journey had begun in my late teens, with some daunting mystical experiences that opened my eyes to a fluid, multidimensional reality. Oddly, I was initiated into animism on a kibbutz while working as a solitary shepherd on Mount Gilboa. My experience there led me to a vegetarian village in northern Israel, where the teachings of Madame Blavatsky and Rudolf Steiner were embraced. Back in America, Kundalini yoga, stringent devotions in a Hindu cult, and marriage to a Christian minister had all taken me further afield from my roots. But while I was painfully disconnected from my family and community, I was also deliciously free from patriarchal dictates and soul-stifling limitations. I was following my own path to God as an undisclosed stranger.

Something uncanny happened when I opened this book. I sensed the author knew me. He was naming, with a verbal scalpel, the fundamentalism I had fled, the male hierarchy that had sent me packing. In its place, *Fragments* seemed to constellate a more expansive *shalshelet*, a soul lineage of those who, like me, yearned for transcendent spaces, and were pursuing a direct experience of the living God.

It did not seem to matter to the author whether one came from a Jewish background or from the spiritual paths of India or Peru, from the Galilee or Brooklyn. He was giving a new voice to the old Hasidic masters, and they were breathing fresh life into the emergent path of awakening. Here they lived happily, side by side with the warm mysticism of Yogananda, the keenness of the Desert Fathers, and the cosmic views of reincarnation and karma. Ramakrishna next to Rebbe Nachman, the *Tibetan Book of the Dead* arm in arm with the Torah of the Baal Shem Tov. Maybe, just maybe, there was some hope here. Maybe I could find refuge in a Judaism large enough to make such equivalences.

When I finally met Reb Zalman in person in 1982, he felt more familiar to me than my own father. He looked at me with his crinkly-wise eyes and said: "*Ergern Nisht!* Don't worry, Tirzah-*leibn*, you aren't alone. The Shekhinah [the feminine aspect of God] is at work here. She's stirring the pot of humanity! How many of us who are questing spiritually have hyphenated identities like you? She is agitating the birth pangs of the planet." Reb Zalman then assured me that there was an entire family of spiritual seekers like me, and invited me to check out his Jewish Renewal movement, which was by then well underway. The rest is history.

In *Fragments of a Future Scroll,* which is a prophetic mishmash of new, paradigm-shifting ideas and devotionally inspired translations of sacred manuscripts, Reb Zalman presents some of the best of what mystical Judaism has to offer the contemporary seeker. Between the covers of this book, we find Judaism re-presented as a blessed path of transcendence into the highest dimensions of the *Eyn Sof*, or the realm of the limitless—as well as a path rooted in the equally blessed dimension of earthly life, where we are called to relish the pleasures of our physical existence and make them holy through ritual, intention, and joy.

You will notice throughout this text that the Kabbalistic jargon (or, as Reb Zalman would later call it, Kabbalese) is still filled with *senex*-speak: old man's language fraught with masculine terms and now outdated binaries. For Reb Zalman, ever on the growing edge of inclusivity, these words would soon evolve as he increasingly learned from and honored his female colleagues, students, and the Feminine Principle Herself.

I celebrate the reissuing of this old friend, which is, like all of us, a work in progress. And I bless you, the reader, to make it your own. Because in translating and bringing us these Hasidic masters as wizardly guides of consciousness, Reb Zalman has reorganized their world to fertilize our own. May we continue to scroll it forward into the future, as we bring forth a Torah for now, one that is spiritually evocative, radically relevant, and surprisingly full of new possibilities—for us and the generations to come.

Rabbi Tirzah Firestone

Boulder, Colorado
December 2024; Kislev 5785

Introduction: Fragments of Renewal

Fools have composed thousands of books of nothingness and emptiness.

—Moses Maimonides, "Letter on Astrology"

Fragments *as an Anti-Book*

Do we expect too much from books? We are taught that they are the touchstones of knowledge, that reading makes one wise, that books are essential for the evolution of humankind. But what can books do, and what can't they do? Do books sometimes get in the way, do they distract us from experiencing the world, do they hide us from ourselves?

Reb Zalman Schachter-Shalomi's *Fragments of a Future Scroll: Hasidism for the Aquarian Age*, first published in 1975, is a book, but it is also a kind of *anti*-book. The book begins with the proclamation "Books and I don't generally get along." And its conclusion ends with the following parting shot:

> Some assume that their book knowledge makes them high. But in truth even the greatest should not take credit for their learning...The patriarchs...observed the entire Torah before it was given...They had "an eye that sees" and "an ear that hears." In contrast to the natural and organic way in which they saw and heard, "your actions are all written in a book" for which you have to see with the eyes of flesh and hear with ears of flesh, and it is all so forced. So, how can anyone whose knowledge comes from books be proud?

The Quran famously refers to the Jews (and Christians) as the "People of the Book." This is offered as a positive gesture, granting Jews and Christians protection that other non-Muslims wouldn't have in Muslim society. But can we also admit that, spiritually speaking, book knowledge is actually a kind of compromise of the patriarchs' and matriarchs' intuitive understanding of what God wants from them? In other words: Are books second-tier sources of knowledge when intuition fails? Are we to infer then, that according to Reb Zalman, books are *not* an end, but a means to recover that which books cannot convey? But of course, the tradition seems to make that kind of "soul retrieval" an epistemological impossibility, part of what the tradition calls "the descent of the generations" (*yeridat hadorot*). According to that line of thinking, books are now all we have, a simulacrum of the true goal of devotion.

The fact that "scroll" is in the title is no accident. *Fragments* is an experiment in returning to some ancient—even imagined—form as a scroll, cuneiform, or codex, on its way to leaving aside books altogether. Reb Zalman writes in the preface:

> Treat this book as a study guide. It is not a textbook. Read a page, think about it, sift the ideas through your consciousness...There are always times when even the best book should be put aside, and you must do your thing. Even the Holy Torah says: "It is time to do something for YHVH (God), leave the Torah aside" (Psalms 119:126).

This is an interesting (mis)reading—or as Harold Bloom would say, misprision—of the verse in Psalms. In the context of the verse, it apparently means, it is "time to act for God" because *they are desecrating Your Torah*: that is, when members of the community, whether the elite or the masses, act against the Torah, then others, whether a prophet or the authorities, must "act for God," in order to protect the Torah. But what does "act for God" mean if not Torah? In the Hasidic text *Mei HaShiloach* (of which Reb Zalman translates a small excerpt in *Fragments*), Mordechai Yosef Leiner of Izbitza makes the provocative antinomian suggestion that sometimes acting for God requires one to abandon (*heferu*) the orbit of halacha (*Torahtekha*, literally "Your Torah").[1] In this instance, the "act of God" is not a stricter adherence to Torah, but its abandonment for the sake of the salvation of its core message. Building upon Leiner, Reb Zalman makes an additional inference that sometimes doing something *for* God requires you to *put down* the book, to "leave the Torah aside," leaving one with the existentially provocative question: When does Torah (i.e., proscribed religion) get in the way of authentically serving, connecting to, or experiencing God?

But of course *Fragments* is, unavoidably, a book. As Reb Zalman writes, "This book has my byline. This only indicates one part of the active channeling of the material...This is not a finished product. The process begins to happen when you, the reader, actualize it in your prayers, meditations, and actions of daily life. *This is spiritual sheet music*."[2]

Here, we are reminded of four things: First, Jean-Paul Sartre's comment in his essay "What Is Literature?" that when the author finishes a book, it is only half done; the other half only happens when the reader reads it. Second, the Trappist monk Thomas Merton's understanding of prose and prayer as intertwined. Third, Nathan of Nemerov's book *Likkutei Tefillot*, which takes each one of his master Rebbe Nachman of Breslov's sermons and makes them into prayers. And finally, we are reminded of the story of the Baal Shem Tov's response when a disciple showed him a text of teachings that he had heard and then transcribed from the Baal Shem himself. The Baal Shem Tov looked at it and allegedly responded, "I do not recognize any of this." In all these cases, the book is an imperfect vehicle at best. And, at least according to the Baal Shem, it is by definition errant.

This is the general trajectory of *Fragments*, the book that is an anti-book that will hopefully one day become a scroll and eventually embed itself into the human heart like the living faith of the patriarchs and matriarchs. It is a book that moves forward as it simultaneously moves backward, reaching for a time before books when teachings were alive with the pulse of speech and feeling. As is the case with any classic, it is a book wholly of its time, and also a book for the ages.

The great Judaic scholar Harry Austryn Wolfson once allegedly said that "writing is an act of sinning and repenting." Ultimately, books only matter when they point the way. If they are things in themselves, if they become sanctified, they cease breathing. Worse, they become idols.

Dawning of the Age

In 1970, the celebrated Jewish historian Yosef Hayim Yerushalmi gave a commencement address, published under the title "A Jewish Historian in an 'Age of Aquarius,'" at Hebrew College in Brookline, Massachusetts. Delivered shortly after the Broadway show *Hair* opened, and as its song "Aquarius" was rising in the music charts, Yerushalmi reflected on how a historian could relate to this seemingly liquid and unconventional moment. In his commencement address, Yerushalmi warned the newly minted graduates of Hebrew College not to underestimate the Age of Aquarius. He wrote:

> The Aquarian mood is essentially an apocalyptic mood and, as such, one which appears and reappears throughout the ages at times of severe historical crisis ... At that point, when those [who] are convinced that the new age has dawned begin to act as though it really had, they generate movements of truly volcanic force, and convulse society to its very foundations.

One could hear the resonance of the sixteenth-century Sabbatean heresy in Yerushalmi's remarks of caution. That would not be an accident, as Yerushalmi published a monograph on Isaac Cardozo, the brother of the famous Sabbatean Abraham Cardozo, in 1971.[3] Yerushalmi expressed extreme caution in his remarks and claimed that it is only the historian who can contextualize and thus temper the mood from spinning out of control. Looking back, it was a reasonable idea. But it was mistaken. The historian may offer much-needed context to understand the present, but historians are neither prophets nor saviors.

Let us also not forget that Yerushalmi's address was delivered two years after the assassinations of Martin Luther King Jr. and Robert F. Kennedy, a few months after the Weather Underground's accidental detonation of a bomb in Greenwich Village on March 6, 1970, and probably only a few weeks after the shooting at Kent State on May 4, 1970, where the National Guard killed four students during an antiwar protest. So, Yerushalmi's worries were not unfounded as he witnessed things unraveling around him, even if his cure may have been short-sighted and self-serving. Yerushalmi, the historian, or what Reb Zalman called "the behaviorist" (more on that below), depicted himself and his guild as the heroic tamers of chaos, cautioning the revolutionaries about the dangers of the Dionysian spirit. This may have been true of Gershom Scholem as well, albeit in a different context. And it was certainly true of Robert Alter in his scathing critique of Arthur Waskow's 1969 Freedom Seder in his essay "Revolutionism and the Jews: 2" in *Commentary*, February 1971.

Countering Yerushalmi and Alter, Reb Zalman embraced the Aquarian Age as a true opportunity for spiritual revival and change—hence the subtitle of the first 1975 edition of *Fragments*, "Hasidism for the Aquarian Age." And while the Aquarian Age did not last and the apocalypse did not arrive, Reb Zalman found a less volatile but no less expressive drive toward spiritual regeneration in the New Age movement that took its place. It is thus not surprising that the 1982 reprint of *Fragments* bears a new subtitle, "Hasidism for the Here and Now." By 1982, the "Aquarian Age" was already dated, but its spirit lived on, and may even be rousing itself now, albeit in unfamiliar and utterly surprising ways.

Such a meta-historical sensibility, coupled with a finely tuned sensitivity to the needs of the moment, came to define Reb Zalman's approach to the dynamics of "renewal." For there are times, Reb Zalman would come to argue in various books and teachings, when leaps in history, or paradigm shifts, initiate dramatic change, requiring a radical reassessment of one's understanding of the world and one's place in it. For Reb Zalman, the three defining moments of the twentieth century, which initiated a planetary transformation that then required a new reality map, were the Holocaust, Hiroshima, and the Moon landing. Each of these uniquely modern events, taken together, urgently challenged humanity to rethink its place in the world, in the cosmos, and in human civilization. The genocidal evil of the Holocaust, the technological evil of Hiroshima, and the realization of global interdependence and ecological fragility conveyed in the iconic image of Earth from outer space—all led Reb Zalman to construct a new model of Jewish participation in the world. In response to what Reb Zalman would refer to as the "fourth turning" of Jewish history, Judaism needed to be reframed as a world religion—not solely for the Jews, but for all of humankind, and Torah recast as a wisdom tradition—not as God's gift to the Jews, but as the Jews' gift to humanity.

Beyond Kiruv*: Jewish Renewal as Revolution, Not Return*

Published in the mid-1970s, in some way *Fragments* is an example of what one might call "*kiruv* literature." *Kiruv rechokim* (bringing back those alienated from Judaism) was a largely postwar American project originating in Orthodoxy to reverse the disaffiliation and assimilation of American Jews by presenting traditional Judaism as a viable and meaningful option for Jewish life in a pluralistic society. (Israel's version was different in numerous ways and not relevant to the project of *Fragments*, which curiously doesn't deal with Israel at all. In 1975 that was still possible.)

Kiruv coalesced around what was called, in the 1970s and 1980s, the *baal teshuvah* movement.[4] Its main architect in postwar America was arguably the Lubavitcher Rebbe, Menachem Mendel Schneerson, who made the movement part of his project of reviving Judaism in postwar America. Figures such as authors Aryeh Kaplan, Gedaliah Fleer (connected to Breslov Hasidism), Shlomo Freifeld (founder of the yeshiva Sh'or Yashuv in Far Rockaway, NY), and many others reframed Hasidism, Kabbalah, and Musar (ethical teachings) through contemporary lenses, in some cases connecting them to meditation and other forms of "Eastern" spirituality, but repackaged for Jewish American seekers. Shlomo Carlebach was certainly integral to that project, as was Reb Zalman early in his career. Carlebach and Reb Zalman served as early emissaries of the sixth Lubavitcher, sent to college campuses to talk to young assimilated Jews about Judaism, beginning their ministry at a Hanukkah party at Brandeis University in its inaugural year, December 1948.[5]

While Carlebach and the others mentioned stayed inside that normative, halachic kiruv project, Reb Zalman began to venture beyond it, especially once the New Age movement gained steam in the early 1970s. In many ways, *Fragments* is his first book-length iteration of his new vision, a kind of breakup letter to the kiruv project. Interestingly, in the early 1970s, a few years before *Fragments* was published, Reb Zalman ended his epistolary communication with the Lubavitcher Rebbe with a strident final letter that was never answered.[6] This rupture makes sense. *Fragments* doesn't want to bring its readers back; it wants to move its readers forward. It is not selling a repackaged tradition through nostalgia, Yiddishkeit, or peoplehood (a term Reb Zalman had little use for), but offers instead a revolutionary new vision of what Judaism *could be*, rather than what it is or has been.

In that register, *Fragments* doesn't faithfully "translate" Kabbalah and Hasidism for a modern audience so much as radically revise both for a new "Aquarian" age. That is, its translation practice is not apologetic or restorative, but revolutionary; one might even call it an act of constructive heresy. It wants to change the tradition it translates as much as change the mind of the one who consumes it. For example, the title of the chapter on Hasidism is called "The Incarnation of the Baal Shem Tov." Reb Zalman knew the term "incarnation" would be dissonant for many Jews at the time, and yet he uses it to describe the Baal Shem Tov to make a point: the Baal Shem Tov was an incarnational figure of sorts, in that he brought back to life something that had "died" within Judaism. The "New Hasidism," as the nascent phenomenon was called at the time, was not something "new," but something "incarnational." Reb Zalman wanted his readers to be both disturbed by the nomenclature and intrigued by its prospects.

As a project of reenvisioning Judaism for the New Age, *Fragments* readily draws from Islam, Christianity, Dharma, and Transcendentalism. "Mitzvah" is translated as "good karma." This playful translation, which also consciously ignores the obligatory nature of the word (literally "to be commanded," *metzuveh*), illustrates that Reb Zalman had something else in mind, which he adapted from Jewish mysticism.[7] A mitzvah, as understood in Kabbalah, is an act that draws divine effluence into the world, an act of attunement that creates goodness while dissipating evil. While it assumes obligation, that is not its focus. Mitzvot, on that reading, are prescribed ways to create good "karma." Such translations are thus not simply tools of communication or terminology to entice the reader; they are experiments meant to convey syncretistic substance. Rooted within an Emersonian and Jamesian worldview in which religious experience is universal, what scholars of the mystical experience sometimes call "pure consciousness" experience, *Fragments* intends not to bring its reader back to Judaism, but to bring a new vision of Judaism to its reader.

Mapping Kabbalism from Tradition to Transformation

One of the most interesting differences between *Fragments* and other kiruv books of its time is that Reb Zalman does not shy away from scholarship. There has often been a tacit tension between kiruv literature and academic Jewish studies scholarship. The former seeks to present an attractive, often overly apologetic rendering of traditional Judaism, which is understandable given that its purpose is selling its reader on halachic Judaism as a prospective life option. Scholarship has a different method and a different end in mind. Scholarship is premised on the production of knowledge and the critique of its subject, often upending conventional ideas and unearthing data that undermines, even subverts, how its subject has been understood through the ambiguous category called Tradition. This is not to say that scholarship doesn't have an agenda (it often does), but in general that agenda is not, nor should it be, aligned with defending Tradition at all costs. Most kiruv literature treats Jewish studies scholarship suspiciously, adopting elements that are not too threatening to its program, and jettisoning anything that challenges its proprietary claims to authority.

Reb Zalman's relationship to scholarship is more complex. Having received a DHL (Doctor of Hebrew Letters) from Hebrew Union College in Cincinnati in 1968, and having taught for years at Temple University in the Department of Religion, Reb Zalman was well-equipped as a scholar. He understood its methods, and its goals. At some point in the 1970s, Reb Zalman decided that academia wasn't for him, largely leaving that world behind. Still, he maintained a belief in the seriousness of the scholarly enterprise and drew from it when it served his more pastoral needs.[8] In some way, Reb Zalman's entire project stands between kiruv and scholarship. Closer to kiruv, Reb Zalman's Renewal program is not founded on the pursuit of truth for its own sake but, rather, on creatively mining the Jewish mystical tradition for the purposes of renewing Jewish spiritual devotion in a new age. Closer to scholarship, Reb Zalman did not want to defend Tradition but, in fact, to transform it. Scholarly method, and some of its findings, were readily used for that spiritual purpose.

In order to elucidate his interdisciplinary approach to received tradition, critical scholarship, and mystical experience, Reb Zalman offers in *Fragments* a tripartite delineation of epistemological character types: the fundamentalist Kabbalist, the behaviorist historian, and the transcendentalist humanist.

The fundamentalist Kabbalist is one who views Kabbalah, traditionally understood, as the exclusive path to the Divine; they fuse Kabbalah with Tradition. (Of course, the term *kabbalah* itself, from the verb "to receive," means, on one reading, "tradition," a clever trick of the mystics.) Reb Zalman writes, "He enters into his consciousness as if it were the only one describing this and other realities. It is largely static. His worlds do not dance freely... Involved in a cosmic battle between the forces of holiness and klippot (shells, the forces of evil), he is solemn and serious and not much in touch with his own body." The fundamentalist Kabbalist carries the cosmos on their shoulders. They do not waver, and they think only within a received body of teachings.

The behaviorist historian steps out of the orbit of what the fundamentalist Kabbalist calls the truly real; in fact, the behaviorist historian calls Kabbalah a myth. They view Kabbalah as the accumulation of humanly constructed doctrines. They know they are "playing a game," and they are willing to portray it as such, yet they "object vigorously to the adept involving *him[self]* in this game." For Reb Zalman, these are largely the academic scholars of Kabbalah. They can be very good teachers and researchers—often better than the fundamentalist Kabbalists, because the behaviorist organizes concepts and categories in ways that are more accessible to non-initiated readers, and because they create scholarly distance between the statements the texts make about themselves and how they might be read—but, existentially speaking, they are prone to miss the forest for the trees.

The Aquarian seeker can benefit from the fundamentalist and behaviorist models, but both will ultimately disappoint them, as they disappointed Reb Zalman. The Aquarian seeker is not looking for "the truth." Rather they are looking "to find in this jungle-like garden of exotic medicinalia a healing for [their] own yearning and dis-ease." The fundamentalists will rarely take the Aquarian seeker seriously, as they are committed to the ironclad interpretation of Kabbalah-as-Tradition, that is, sacred in a doctrinal sense. And the Aquarian seeker will also be disappointed by the horizontal nature of the behaviorist model, because the behaviorist does not sufficiently recognize the transcendent realm *prima facie* that the Aquarian seeker desires to commune with. Thus, Reb Zalman argues, the Aquarian seeker requires a new method, a new paradigm, a new approach. He calls this the approach of the "humanistic transcendentalist."

The humanistic transcendentalist desires what the fundamentalist wants, but not on their terms and conditions. And they need what the behaviorist has, but cannot accept their premises, nor their goals. The "future scroll" will take both and refract them through the Aquarian desire for wholeness that does not maintain a bifurcated body and spirit and refuses the rigid rationalism of the historical claim by maintaining that the human can also house the Divine.

Translation as a Devotional Act of Renewal

Fragments is a Jewish book, but not a book written only for Jews. In fact, the Aquarian Age begins to deconstruct the very categories of Jew and gentile by offering a third case, the one who seeks to encounter the Divine—call it YHVH, Christ, Krishna, Buddha, or something else. In his book *Radical Judaism*, Arthur Green draws a distinction between the concepts of "Jew" and "Israel." Jews, as such, are those born of Jewish parentage. "Israel" refers to all those who are seekers of the One God.[9]

Reb Zalman might agree. In some way, Reb Zalman envisioned Renewal as a Jewish gift to the Aquarian world, its particular iteration of "Israel," in the most spiritualized sense. *Fragments* is thus written for a broad community of seekers, both Jews and non-Jews alike. Just as Martin Buber wanted his Christian and philosopher friends in Germany to recognize the "orientalism" of Judaism, Reb Zalman wanted his readers to see the spiritual/New Age resources of the Jewish tradition as a refraction of and complement to all other world wisdom traditions. This in fact became one of the primary reorientations of Reb Zalman's project of Renewal: the development of an "organismic" approach to world religions, in which the planet is understood as a single body, with each of the world's religions being a particular organ within that earthly whole. The fundamentalist Kabbalist would likely call it heresy, and the behaviorist historian would likely call it a waste of time. But for the humanistic transcendentalist, it was an authentic exercise in innovation (*chidush*).

In this sense, Renewal is a translational project of epic existential proportions—texts and languages, paradigms and practices, maps and symbols, stories and experiences—all undergoing various degrees of transformation for the very Aquarian purpose of expanding consciousness and elevating human life in tune with the paradigmatic shifts of the late twentieth century. Accordingly, the entire second half of *Fragments* is dedicated to a collection of highly idiosyncratic translations of various texts. These translations are more than mere excerpts from "the greatest hits" of the Jewish mystical tradition. Rather, they represent a carefully curated collection of texts that illustrate the kind of humanistic mystical Judaism that Reb Zalman both embodied and taught. Given the significant space Reb Zalman dedicated to such translations in *Fragments* (at least half of the book), as well as his voluminous translational work that continued throughout the next four decades, one might consider: How does Reb Zalman's concept and practice of translation function, both poetically and spiritually, in *Fragments* as well as in his decades-long work of Renewal?

In his essay "The Task of the Translator," Walter Benjamin writes that "translation is a mode." By this he means (as he elaborates further on in the essay) that "a specific significance inherent in the original manifests itself in its translatability."[10] Translatability is thus a quality wherein something embedded in potential awaits actualization by the hand of the translator. For Benjamin, translations do not simply convey information or data (he calls that "bad translation"); they are more than the convergence of two languages. Rather, translations reveal aspects of the original text that were heretofore concealed, giving expression to what Benjamin calls the original's "afterlife." "In translation the original rises into a higher and purer linguistic air, as it were."[11] Translation does not merely convey, but gives new life; it pushes the original into places the original did not, could not, go.

Benjamin uses two terms to describe translation that should catch our attention regarding Reb Zalman's Renewal project: the first is "echo," and the second is "harmony." On echo, Benjamin writes, "The task of the translator consists in finding the particular intention toward the target language which produces in that language the echo of the original." And on harmony, "the language of a translation can—in fact, must—let itself go, so that it gives voice to the *intentio* of the original not as reproduction but as harmony, as a supplement to the language in which it expresses itself, as its own kind of *intentio*."[12]

Both echo and harmony are supplements. An echo reverberates, usually produced by sound bouncing off an object (e.g., a mountain, a valley, a wall). It reproduces the sound through repetition but also distorts the original, often in evocative and expansive ways. Harmony is the combination of playing one note over another simultaneously, expanding the original sound, broadening and deepening its resonance. Harmony is manifest in two ways: consonance and dissonance. The first produces a pleasing sound, the second, a kind of tension. Good translation should do both; it can introduce the reader to the beauty of the original, and it can disturb the reader by the incongruity between the original and the new context in which it is now being read. This blend of consonance and dissonance lies at the core of Renewal as Reb Zalman envisioned it. Reb Zalman doesn't try to overly beautify the texts he translates, and here he differs from kiruv literature, which sought to smooth over as many cracks and round as many edges as possible. Rather, he produces a kind of harmonic consonance and dissonance to accompany the melody of the original as it echoes through time.

Reb Zalman viewed translation as both spiritual practice and art form, expressing an ethos as well as an aesthetics, and he translated myriad texts throughout his career, such as the Hasidic poems and prayers of Ahrele Roth (the founder of the Toldot Aaron Hasidic sect), the Yiddish poetry of Abraham Joshua Heschel, and many dozens of Psalms.[13] He left behind unpublished translations of Rilke's poetry into Hebrew, and one of *Yedid Nefesh* (the Hebrew liturgical poem) that he had translated into German. He also translated some Romantic English poetry into Hebrew. It seems that Reb Zalman viewed translation, like Benjamin, as a radical act of disclosure, as a sacred dance between fidelity and freedom. Translation, not unlike commentary, is a key to unlocking the original, linguistically sealed inside itself.

Most importantly for practitioners (not just scholars or armchair mystics), Reb Zalman urged his readers to chant his translations, to recite them "out loud," as mystics have chanted Psalms, or the Song of Songs, or Rumi's poetry, or Gregorian chants, or the Upanishads for millennia. He wanted his translations to come alive as devotional literature, for the reader/reciter to discover themselves in the experiential echo of the text. Like Buber (who began his work on Hasidism with translations), Reb Zalman understood translation as more than introductory; it was also setting the stage for a new project of religiosity, a new lens through which to view an age-old tradition.[14] He writes, "The task of re-discovering the Aquarian materials in Jewish mysticism has not even begun in a systematic way. But systematic is Piscean anyhow; and organic is Aquarian."

Both Benjamin and Reb Zalman believed that translation must seek to reproduce and transform simultaneously. As such, we can understand Reb Zalman's deep investment in translation as a methodological template of Renewal, and the reason I think he devoted half of *Fragments* to his harmonious translations of these transformative texts. Here Reb Zalman is both innovator and traditionalist, seeking to conserve the original by freeing it.

The End of the Beginning

In 1975, feminism was just beginning to appear on the horizon of progressive Judaism. It would eventually play a crucial role in Renewal, and the early movement would later change its name from Bnai 'Or (Sons of Light) to Pnei 'Or (Faces of Light). One feels that, in *Fragments*, Reb Zalman is just beginning to explore the role of feminism in his evolving project. By the early 1980s, Renewal would become a vanguard of feminist Judaism. In *Fragments*, we see the first glimpses of that development.

We are now half a century past the culture and context that gave birth to *Fragments*. And today, a new iteration of Jewish radicalism and renewal is emerging: religiously audacious, politically activist, and in search of new ways to formulate, integrate, and conceptualize what it means to be a Jew in the twenty-first century. Rethinking diaspora in a time of ascendant nationalism, revising consciousness in a world of techno-mania and artificial intelligence. In this rapidly changing environment, *Fragments* is certainly a "blast from the past." But as any valuable piece of literature, it is also a signpost, or even a GPS, for the future. Reprinting this edition on the fiftieth anniversary of its original publication is not meant as an act of nostalgia or as a purely historical exercise. We believe that *Fragments* still has something to offer—its critique, its innovation, and its commitment to experimentation.

As the reader embarks on reading or rereading *Fragments* today, it is worth remembering, and also forgetting, its context. Let it speak to you as it spoke to us when it first appeared. Today we can look at it through the prism of a larger body of work, and we can see the sparks that would later become the fire of Renewal. There are books that are worth rereading periodically—not to remember what was forgotten, but to remind ourselves why it was worth remembering them in the first place. *Fragments of a Future Scroll* is one of those books.

·

I was recently in Washington Square Park and noticed a young couple sitting and intently reading a book together. As I approached them, I realized they were reading Ram Dass's *Be Here Now*, first published in 1971. I said to them, "I first read that book over forty years ago. I'm really happy to see people reading it now." They looked at me, appreciative but a bit confused, not quite sure how to respond to this friendly Boomer. As I walked away I noticed they immediately dove back into Ram Dass's evocative and allusive words. I smiled and thought, *this is how traditions are made*.

Rabbi Shaul Magid

Thetford, Vermont
February 2025; Shevat 5785

NOTES

1 Leiner's *chidush* (innovation) is in reading the verb "abandon" (*heferu*) not as the abandonment of Torah (in the negative) but rather as an "act of God" that sometimes requires an abandonment of Torah in order to save Torah.

2 Italics are mine.

3 Yosef Hayim Yerushalmi, *From Spanish Court to Italian Ghetto: Isaac Cardoso, a Study in Seventeenth-Century Marranism and Jewish Apologetics* (Columbia University Press, 1971).

4 For more on the baal teshuvah movement, see Sarah Benor, *Becoming Frum: How Newcomers Learn the Language and Culture of Orthodox Judaism* (2012) and Janet Aviad, *Return to Judaism: Religious Renewal in Israel* (1983).

5 Arthur Green, not in the Orthodox camp, contributed to this use of Hasidism as a form of kiruv as a tool of inspiration for young seekers of spirituality in Judaism.

6 Interestingly, and intentionally, he wrote the letter on Reconstructionist Rabbinical College stationery.

7 Here one can also see connections to Mordecai Kaplan's notion of the mitzvot as "folkways," an influence Reb Zalman readily acknowledges, as well as to the American Reform movement's characterization of mitzvot as "good deeds."

8 One chapter in *Fragments* illustrates this dynamic in practice. Reb Zalman traveled to Jerusalem in the early 1960s and studied with Gershom Scholem, the famed historian of Kabbalah. He drew much from Scholem's writings, reworking them toward New Age renewal ends that Scholem may not have agreed with. In his chapter on Kabbalah in *Fragments*, Reb Zalman draws heavily from Scholem's lengthy essay in *Encyclopedia Judaica* (mentioned at the beginning of the chapter) that was later published as an independent volume titled *Kabbalah*. And in an unpublished series of lectures delivered at Bryn Mawr College in 1991, titled "Renewal Is Not Heresy: Where We Differ from Sabbateanism," Reb Zalman draws heavily from Scholem's work on Sabbatai Zevi. (A much-abbreviated version of the lectures at Bryn Mawr was published under the title *Renewal NOW*.)

9 Arthur Green, *Radical Judaism: Rethinking God and Tradition* (Yale University Press, 2010), 131–149.

10 Walter Benjamin, "The Task of the Translator," in *Illuminations: Essays and Reflections*, trans. Harry Zohn and ed. Hannah Arendt (Schocken Books, 2007), 70–71.

11 Benjamin, "Task of the Translator," 75.

12 Walter Benjamin, "The Task of the Translator," in *Walter Benjamin: Selected Writings Volume 1, 1913–1926*, eds. Marcus Bullock and Michael W. Jennings (Belknap Press, 1996), 258–60.

13 Zalman Schachter-Shalomi and Yair Hillel Goelman eds., *Ahron's Heart: The Prayers, Teachings, and Letters of Ahrele Roth: A Hasidic Reformer* (Ben Yehuda Press, 2009); *Psalms in a Translation for Praying* (The Alliance of Jewish Renewal, 2014); Abraham Joshua Heschel, *Human: God's Ineffable Name*, trans. Zalman Schachter-Shalomi (Albion-Andalus Books, 2012). Zalman translated Heschel's poems as a gift to Heschel, his mentor, in 1969, but Heschel died before they could finalize the translations. Zalman revised and published the translations in 2012.

14 For Martin Buber's early translations of Hasidic tales, see Buber, *The Tales of Rabbi Nachman* (Humanities Press, 1956).

Preface from the 1975 Edition

Treat this book as a study guide. It is not a textbook. Read a page, think about it, sift the ideas through your consciousness. Let what comes from your mind float free, and follow gently. More than what stimulated it, your own production is what counts in spiritual life.

There are always times when even the best book should be put aside, and you must do your thing. Even the Holy Torah[1] says: "It is time to do something for *YHVH* (God), leave the Torah aside" (Psalms 119:126). As you will see, we start by admitting the uselessness of books, and end on the same note. This book won't do a thing for you. But your response to it can do everything, with God's grace and the higher mind which is your own.

There are, these days, very few viable models for the seeker to follow. In this waking age, we must forge our own. "Forge" has a double meaning. We forge firm constructions out of metal brought to white heat then beaten into shape, but a forgery is also a fake. Another generation, anchored in the consciousness of the past, might call a forgery what you, the seeker, are attempting. From that perspective, it is true. But this attitude no longer provides useful road maps for our time. Today we must blaze our own trails.

Why bother, then, to write a book containing so much material from the past? After you begin this spiritual work, you'll clearly see that we all come from some place. And it is a deep place. Remember the shelves in the bookstore where this book was offered? Many are the treasures from the past there on display. They are all of help to some people. They have helped me. Chances are that if some of them hadn't helped you before, you would not hold this book in your hand now. So, treat this as a forging tool.

The way this book happened may interest you. Most of this material comes from awareness classes and classes in Jewish mysticism. In these, I might read a holy text from the past. Its content sparked lights in me, and my students. I translated it. The material included here represents about two percent of these translated teachings. Other material came into print from excerpts of yet unpublished larger works that seemed helpful to the students, myself, my editors, or my publisher. At times the editors wrote introductory or connecting passages.

Realize that much of what happens in these pages is the result of a rich tradition of teaching. There's still a lot of mileage in it. As you ascend, you'll see this for yourself. In all spiritual recipes, the proof is the result. Let your higher mind guide you to reinterpret some of the material which at first turns you off. You will find the way in which *your* light will discern the intention and illumination as perceived by an earlier sage or saint.

This book has my byline. This only indicates one part of the active channeling of the material. All the good in it is Divine Mind that was active in seer, sage, and saint who came before. Stimulated by my listeners and readers, this handbook happened with the help of associates visible in this realm like Pip Mandelkorn and Steve Gerstman. Sometimes it seemed other, helpful souls peeked over our shoulders and worked through our minds, guiding us from planes meshing with our own.

This is not a finished product. The process begins to happen when you, the reader, actualize it in your prayers, meditations, and actions of daily life. This is spiritual sheet music. It is not meant to be a completed concerto, but spiritual finger exercises; a primer to make it possible to tackle a text. It is an hors d'oeuvre to keep the seeker from starving until a decent meal can be prepared.

We hope to receive your responses and be guided by them in later editions. In reading this study guide, you take responsibility too. If you find flaws in anything from the teachings to typesetting, or language choice, advise us. And please keep us in your prayers.

Zalman M. Schachter

Winnipeg, Manitoba
November 14, 1973; 19th of Cheshvan 5734

Yahrzeit of Reb Yakov of Husyatin in the week that we read "and he did make them a feast and they did eat and drink."

NOTE

1 Torah: literally "the Guidance," or "the Teachings." In a narrow sense, the Torah refers to the Five Books of Moses (the Chumash). In a wider sense, the Torah comprises both the Written Law (the twenty-four books of the Bible, or the Tanakh) and the Oral Law (the Talmud). Defined wider yet, the Torah is perceived as all Jewish sacred literature. For some, Torah means the will and wisdom of God in all times and places.

AQUARIAN TEACHINGS

Introduction to Part One

Books and I don't generally get along. Two differing attitudes underlie my way of teaching and the way of writing a book. As a teacher, I'm notoriously untrustworthy on class descriptions. This is because I teach people, not subjects. Were I to teach a subject, I would begin with a plan in which definitions, concepts, premises, and methods would all come at the beginning. The center of the course would be divided into neat chapter headings, and it would end with a fairly clear summary of what went on before.

But I see myself as a resource person who brings to the students shelves from a supermarket of experience and ideas. As a guide for their appetites, digestion, and needs, I can only echo the sages of the Talmud who declare that there is no order of precedence, "no earlier and later in Torah."

All that happens in the mind depends upon valences born of interests, needs, and concerns in the student or seeker. As an instrument in the hands of the Spirit who informs and guides, I permit this life force to play on whichever key it wills. The best preparation on my part is to be well-informed, open, available, and sensitive to the transactions that take place in the interpersonal realm. It is not my intention to interfere with the process of the Beit HaMidrash, the "House of Searching Study."

I have gained much from books when, as I brought my concerns and conditions to them, I let them speak to those very concerns and conditions. If hard-pressed to explain what the author's original idea was, there were times I could not have responded meaningfully. Still, it is true for me to say that authors have seeded, fertilized, and cultivated ideas that were to shape my life. The process is one in which the Self instructs the self, utilizing texts as well as insights in the process.

Reb Pinchas of Koretz[1] interprets the verse "the soul of man teaches him knowledge" by raising the question: If the soul of man teaches him all his life, then why is anyone still ignorant when he dies? And he answers his own question: This is because the soul is not a good drillmaster. It never repeats itself. So the bright light of insight, if it is never repeated, vanishes and is lost. "And thou shalt teach your children diligently," thus repeating important truths until they become a part of life itself. He also cautioned on speaking of important seed insights until they have ripened. Spoken prematurely, they may be stillborn.

This book is a record of some of those enlightening shafts of light, to read, hopefully reread, ponder and meditate upon, and to apply in daily life. The proof of truth will come to the reader as the teachings of his own soul are resurrected. As Moshe Chaim Luzzatto[2] put it: "I have not come to teach the reader anything new, but to recall to mind that which is well-known to him."

On one of my journeys to Chicago, I was to meet with a group and conduct a meditation session. I wanted to buy some incense sticks, and as this was in the early 1960s (before head shops), I knew of only a few outlets for joss sticks. Certain that I could always find some at the Vedanta Society, I called the Ramakrishna-Vivekananda Mission and introduced myself to the Swami. He said: "You Jews are such a spiritual people." I was puzzled by this and asked him how he meant that. "Everywhere I go," the Swami replied, "Baha'i, Vedanta, Subud, Zen, Theosophical Society...they are full of Jews!" I was filled with both joy and dismay at this, for I knew it was so. The more spiritual the Jew, the more difficult it seems for him or her to find a place in the synagogue. This is largely so because many synagogues project images of God, Torah, and the Sabbath that allow little room for the celebration of the spirit moving many people in the new age. It is no wonder that Jews drift to other places in search of a celebration more resonant to their sensibilities and more aligned with their values.

Jewish mysticism, it has been said, is fine for those who are deeply immersed in the halachic[3] life and thus have reached the plateau attainable by the normative means of piety. Having "filled their belly with Talmud," and reached the age of forty, they are deemed capable of entering into the mysteries of Judaism. But, for those unqualified to enter into this study, other ways are suggested: Kashrut (eating Kosher), Tefillin (daily prayer), Shabbat (Sabbath observance), and many other rituals, with the emphasis falling on the letter of the law. Yet, to those who seem unable or unwilling to follow the "empty rituals," little of substance has been offered. It is no wonder that so many are leaving in the midst of such polarization—leaving to nurture the tender shoots of youthful spiritual insights in what appears to be more fertile soil.

For there is no denying the current interest of Jews in mysticism. Even secular Jewish literature shows an involvement in mysticism at one level or another (consider Elie Wiesel, I. B. Singer, or Franz Kafka). It is now a part of our general education to know the ideas and principles of Eastern teachings, in one form or another, which pervade contemporary culture. Still, the Jewish establishment is mainly unprepared to meet the new demands that this new consciousness calls for. Having been trained at a time when Dewey and Whitehead were in vogue, they have difficulty in discussing Teilhard de Chardin, Buckminster Fuller, or D. T. Suzuki in a Jewish context. It would be difficult to find a rabbi conversant enough with the Jewish counterparts of Tarot, transcendental meditation, I Ching, or astrology, for example, to be able to discuss them with the young seeker.

Youth, as a matter of fact, is not waiting for understanding or approbation. The counterculture is a reality, with its own understanding about itself, life, and the Divine. There are a few (one might call them revolutionaries or reformers) who are insisting that there is a Jewish expression to spiritual needs. One finds people chanting the Shema like a mantra. In Esalen-like growth centers, people wrapped in tallitot (prayer shawls) sway in rapture and chant from a siddur (prayer book) and dance with great joy to greet the Shabbat. *Chavurot* (informal prayer and study groups; literally "fellowships") are giving courses in the texts of Jewish mysticism, which are received with great interest by their members and the community outside. At Rabbi Shlomo Carlebach's House of Love and Prayer in San Francisco, young people are learning and meditating in a Jewish context. Many of them have come from other communes where the exciting rumor of Jewish mysticism had reached them. In New York, Rabbi Joseph Gelberman conducts services and gives counsel and instruction according to his insights in Hasidism and Kabbalah.

I do not consider it to be dangerous for persons of Jewish background to experience and explore Eastern mysticism, provided they check it out for technique and content, rather than for ritual, dogma, and ethnic identity. The process of a soul's way to God is often initiated by an excursion into the realms of the Eastern religions. Of the forms of yoga available, hatha yoga is surely no problem. But bhakti yoga may become a problem, especially as it relates to forms like Krishna consciousness and the Hare Krishna movement since the followers of the teacher Bhaktivedanta are asked for exclusive devotion and must deny all other religious ways. Satchitananda is a warm teacher, appreciative of the Jewish way and encouraging people to find themselves in Judaism. Ramakrishna-Vivekananda people are generally helpful to Jews, as are Yogananda's followers. Zen can be helpful, especially the way it is taught at the San Francisco Zen Center and Tassajara; Roshi Baker is a very caring man. Wali Ali of the San Francisco Sufis, himself a Jew, and the disciple of the late (Jewish) Sufi Sam Lewis, and Yogi Bhajan are friendly, and encourage their followers to deepen their Jewish experience.

I see the greatest problem in the fact that once the spiritual progress is initiated in the Jewish seeker, he, in order to integrate the experience into his life, finds no place where he might do so with other Jews. If Jewish leaders and communities reject these Jews, we reject the finest, most sensitive, and spiritual persons of our age.

NOTES

1 Reb Pinchas was a spiritual Hasidic master of eighteenth-century Europe.
2 Moshe Chaim Luzzatto (1707–1747), also known as the Ramchal, was an Italian Kabbalist and poet.
3 Halacha is the Hebrew term for Jewish Law. The many laws and rules that apply to the Jew have been derived by Talmudic scholars from the Torah. Though observing the halacha fairly uniformly, over the centuries Jews have interpreted the halacha differently, according to the traditions they accept and follow, or according to their inner conviction. Kabbalists and Jewish mystics have taken halacha in a mystical, sometimes sacramental way, understanding the performance of the mitzvot (the commandments) to have a spiritual value on many interlocking levels. The Baal Shem Tov taught that the halachic way of life is intended to be joyful, fervent, spiritual, and uplifting.

Hasidism: The Incarnation of the Baal Shem Tov

Over two hundred years ago, in Podolia, a small place in Russia, where Russia, Turkey, and Poland meet, near the Carpathian Mountains, the Baal Shem Tov (or Besht, an acronym), whose name means "Master of the Good Name," began the movement known as Hasidism. Hasidim (the followers of the Besht) were fond of saying that when God saw the Children of Israel would be unable to last until the coming of the *Mashiach* (Messiah), because they had grown faint and almost despaired of Heaven, He took a bit of the effulgence of Mashiach, embedded it in the soul of the Besht, and gave us something to help see us through. The conditions of the Jews in seventeenth-century Europe have been described many times: how not long before the Cossack Chmelnitsky had led his hordes through town after town, massacring hundreds of thousands of Jews; how twice, in a very short time, false Messiahs had risen up, raising hopes, and then smashing them. Hasidism—the way of joy and devotion—looked toward the future, instructing not so much "what," but "how."

The Baal Shem Tov, whose given name was Israel, son of Eliezer and Sarah, began his ministry in 1734 at the age of thirty-six. The appellation "Baal Shem Tov" is supposed to mean that he was a miracle worker. He was capable of using the Divine Name (the "Good Name") for purposes of changing things from what they are to what they ought to be; because there is always such a discrepancy between how things are and how they ought to be. His greatest miracle, of course, was to take a human being who had almost completely given up and bring him back to life; to take a person who had despaired of being able to attain anything spiritual or divine in this world and infuse him with spirit, to show him that the possibility was still there, and what is more important, to show him how he can achieve it.

Martin Buber relates how excited he was when he came upon the text where the Besht says "and he rises like a new man, capable of truly begetting." Buber rediscovered precisely this virility of spirit through the writings of the Besht. This "know-how" counseling on how to live, not just study, a truly spiritual life is what concerned him. And for us—if there are teachings available to us, then we ought to know what they are and learn how to follow them as well.

What is Hasidism all about? It is a way, a moving way. It is a way of serving God. Man has to be freed and to regain his ability to dream his dream. The late Lubavitcher Rebbe told us once that his grandfather, the Rebbe Shmuel, the Maharash of Lubavitch, said that every human being ought to pretend for at least half an hour, once in a while, that he is a perfect tzadik (righteous person, saint).

There is not a single one of us who could not give advice to the whole world as to *what* it ought to do. The only problem is *how?* It's like when the thief gives someone a recipe for an omelet. He doesn't just say, "first, you take two eggs," for where are we going to take them from? He says instead, "first, you go and steal two eggs," because that is how he knows to make an omelet. The problem is always the know-how.

What the Baal Shem did, then, and all his followers after him, was not tell us what to do. In fact, regarding the *what*, he did not change anything. What he did was to tell them *how*.

In a *ma'aseh* (a Hasidic tale) retold by Martin Buber, a disciple of Reb Moshe of Kobryn was asked, after the death of his master, what was most important to his teacher. He replied, "Whatever he happened to be doing at the moment." Hasidic teachers, from the Besht on, taught by their example. For this reason, stories about their actions, conversations, miracles, comments, and commentaries, and their own stories and parables, were told and retold by those who were seeking the know-how. That this was a knowledge both spiritual and practical is illustrated by the ma'aseh of the disciple who upon being asked why he had traveled such a long way to be with his teacher, immediately replied, "To watch how he ties his shoes."

The flavor of Hasidism is contained in the ma'aseh. To give one example:

> Once there was a man who decided he was going to follow the disciples of Reb Mendel of Kotzk. He came to Kotzk and was right away put to a test. Nobody, of course, was to tell him how the test was to be conducted. The first morning, all the other Kotzker Hasidim got up very early, finished davening (praying), but did not tell the new man. He got up at seven o'clock, thinking that he was up very early, only to find the rest back on their benches, making out to be asleep. He knew that they did not make such a fuss about davening in Kotzk, and so he waited to see what would happen.
>
> Soon, the Hasidim woke up, and said to him: "Come, let's get something to eat before we daven." Now the young man had never in his life eaten before making his morning prayers, and this confused him. When he protested, they shrugged their shoulders, saying, "He wants to be a Hasid and does not eat before davening!" Finally, after much pressuring, one of the Hasidim said, "Look, we'll go to the very old, venerable Hasid with the long beard, and whatever he says, you'll do." The young man agreed, and he went to the old man. The old man said: "Of course, everybody says to eat; don't be a fool! Sit down and eat!"
>
> And so they gave him wine and cake, and he began to make the *brakhah* (blessing), but before he said God's name, they grabbed him, put him on the table, and started yelling at him, "Ha! You take the word of a human being just because the old goat has a long beard! For that you will sell your God short?" And so the young Hasid received his first lesson.

Life Here and After

Death did not frighten the pious Jew of old. He had faith in the Talmud and its statement that death is a transition from one life into another, as easy as removing a strand of hair from a glass of milk. What the Jew wanted above all was to die fully conscious, in full possession of his mind at the time that his soul left his body. Deathbed scenes abound in Hasidic literature, and were favorites for retelling in Hasidic circles.

Hasidim often prepared themselves for death by asking the rebbe for advice on how to meditate at the moment of their passing. They were convinced that they could serve the same One God in many worlds and looked forward even to *Gehinom* as a place of service. The Jewish idea of Gehinom is not hell, but rather a purgatory where the soul is purged from all defilement that has accumulated during its life on earth. Reb Zushia of Annipol once said that if God were to command him to go to Gehinom, he would gird his loins and jump down with glee to fulfill the divine command.

The soul that has become too fully and too completely identified with the body through sensual indulgence is unable to separate from it. To accompany the body to its final resting place and to behold its putrefaction and decay is painful for such souls. This is what is known as *chibbut hakever*,[1] the pain and anguish of the grave. To destroy the illusory identification of the soul with the body, and to avert such pain, many Hasidim prepare themselves during life on earth by ascetic practices. Exalted souls are able to achieve the same end through prayer or meditation. They become oblivious of their physical body and surroundings. These practices are consistent with the teaching, espoused in numerous world traditions, to "die before you die."

If the soul cannot rid itself of its earthly images and desires, its "dust," it is forced to wander earthbound for ages, in limbo, in a world of emptiness. In one Hasidic tale, a lost soul who has already roamed for hundreds of years in such a void cries out, "Would that I already had reached Gehenna!"[2] In order to reach Gehinom, the soul must already be purified from illusion. Purgatory was often described in lurid physical details of fire and cold. Yet, the Rebbes warn against the error of seeing Gehinom as a physical place. It is rather like the pain of anxiety, intensified by silence and a deep awareness of the evil one has committed. According to tradition, Gehinom is emptied on the Sabbath, which has led to interpretations that this respite is granted only to those who keep the Sabbath in this life. Others disagree, saying that Gehinom is emptied for all, regardless of their level of religious observance. If not for the weekly bliss and light that the Sabbath provides, the soul would not be able to bear the anguish of Gehinom.

When a soul is ready to enter *Gan Eden* (Paradise, literally the Garden of Eden), it must first be immersed in the river of light that flows from the fervent perspiration of the heavenly hosts as they sing glory to the Most High. The immersion is to empty the soul of remaining earthly images so that it may, without further illusions, see heaven for what it really is.

The soul first enters the lower Gan Eden, which is a paradise of emotional bliss. While on earth, most people are unable to feel more than one dominant emotion at a time, but the bliss of the souls in the lower Gan Eden is likened to a majestic chord of benign emotions which the soul feels toward God and toward other souls.

In the Hasidic view (as well as the Swedenborgian, as it happens), heaven is organized into societies. Those with mutual interests in Torah and divine service are drawn together where they can serve His Blessed Name according to their own specialty and individuality. Each heavenly society is taught by its rabbi and led on to further celestial attainment. Thus, the lower Gan Eden is the heaven of emotional fervor.

Before a soul is raised from the lower to the higher Gan Eden, it must again immerse itself in the river of light so that it will forget and forsake the fervor of the emotions for the delights of knowing God through understanding. To serve God with insight, through the study of Torah and with love of the mind, is its own reward. The societies of the upper Gan Eden are organized into yeshivot (schools of study), which pursue an ever-deepening understanding of the Divine Mind as it is invested in Torah. Each day at midnight, the Holy One, Blessed Be He, Himself appears, and enters Gan Eden to delight in sharing His Blessed Wisdom with the righteous who have gained the upper Gan Eden.

Nothing new can be gained by a person in heaven. The balance of mitzvot (commandments, good karma) and Torah at the time of death is what remains with a person after death. In heaven, he gains only a deeper and richer understanding of his life on earth. It is for that reason that souls, once they have absorbed all that heaven has to offer, request reincarnation, in order to achieve further perfection. Reincarnation is also granted to allow the soul to bring about restitution of the wrongs it has committed. Thus, reincarnation can come after Gehinom, after the lower paradise or after the higher paradise.

This process goes on until a soul has fully built its own spiritual body. The idea of the spiritual body hearkens back to the time of the Mishnah.[3] The Talmud tells us that Rabbi Judah the Prince, the compiler of the Mishnah, returned in a spiritual body every Sabbath eve to his family to sanctify the Sabbath by celebrating the kiddush with them. He did this for an entire year. It was only when one of the servants of the family revealed this to neighbors, that Judah the Prince took leave of his family never to return again on the grounds that his coming would put other saints to shame. Thus, Judah the Prince had attained the fullness of the spiritual body in his last incarnation on earth.

And yet, even the completion of the spiritual body is not the ultimate state of being. Having attained such fullness, a soul can be "absorbed into the very Body of the King," the ultimate aim of its yearning and longing. Thus the soul merges finally in God, as a drop in the ocean.

Just as the *Tibetan Book of the Dead* is not only a funeral manual but also—and this today is its more important function—a guide for spiritual attainment, so too are these Jewish teachings a guide for spiritual purgation and attainment of the blessed state for us living today.

NOTES

1 In Hebrew: חיבוט הקבר.
2 Gehinom in Yiddish.
3 The Mishnah was the first part of the Oral Law to be written down. The Talmud, written down centuries later, is composed of the Mishnah and the Gemara, which consists of commentaries on the Mishnah and many other teachings.

The Spiritual Guide

In the Hasidic Rebbes of the eighteenth, nineteenth, and twentieth centuries, the Jewish spiritual guide reached a high level of sophistication. Not that spiritual direction waited till the eighteenth century. The priests and prophets of old were charged with teaching the fold the deeds that they shall do. Prophets Ezra and Nehemiah were guides not only of a nation, but also of individuals and groups. Contemporaneous with the Dead Sea community, the Pharisees (much maligned and misunderstood) were also guides, ultimately forming the model for the Desert Fathers of the Christians.

After the holocausts of the years 70 and 130 BCE, some mystics became guides, mapping the regions of heaven and hell, prescribing for their disciples the way to the former, and the best means of avoiding the latter. In the twelfth century, the Friends of God in the Rheinland, a group of Catholic pietists, worked side by side with the *Hasidei Ashkenaz* (the Pious of Ashkenaz) in present-day Germany, a community under the spiritual direction of Judah the Hasid (or Judah the Pious) of Ratisbon and the disciples he raised to continue his work. Alongside the Christian mystics, several circles of Jewish mystics operated in Spain, as well as in Provence, France in the Middle Ages. Their counsels are basically those found in the Zohar literature and collated in the work of Elijah De Vidas in the sixteenth century.[1]

The guide had reached a level of immense sanctity by the sixteenth century, especially in the circle of Safed in Galilee, where they were operating in the realm of trance and astral travel. The power to communicate with Elijah had become common among the disciples of Isaac Luria and Chaim Vital.[2] In the sixteenth century, Isaiah Horowitz and Judah Loeb of Prague (associated with the Golem stories) reached great heights of mystical abilities and each had his circle of disciples. The two pseudo-messiahs, Sabbatai Tzvi and Jacob Frank, had so many followers that their failures created a great crisis in Jewish life.

These guides acted as the osmotic channels of the esoteric teachings, passing them on to their own disciples, but otherwise not engaging in transforming society or widening the process in any significant way. All this changed with the Baal Shem Tov. Some of the greatest souls among his contemporaries became his disciples. The Besht's disciples, and his disciples' disciples, became the founders of Hasidic dynasties of charismatic leaders. Their ministry had as its central task the spiritual direction of their Hasidim who came from afar, spending weeks or years at the feet of their masters, listening to their public discourses and seeking private counsel.

Basic to the Hasidic Rebbe's orientation was the Besht's teaching:

> The ways of the Lord are straightforward. There are many ways. God wishes to be served in all ways. Sometimes in this way, sometimes in another. When a person finds his path blocked, this may mean that God now wishes to be served in another manner. Do not despise any man for his kind of service; for all ways lead to Him.

The Rebbes did not just deal with persons of highly dedicated caliber, but with all kinds of people from every walk of life. So great was their influence that almost all of Eastern European Jewry became one large spiritual community. The Hasidic community in each town became the place of ecstatic transport to God. The fellowship of the Hasidim was of immense depth. They encouraged and reinforced each other's commitment. With ruthless honesty, they shared not only their virtues, but also the afflictions of their hearts.

The Rebbe did not so much intermediate between the Hasid

and God as merge himself and the Hasid in the Infinite One. The Hasid made the momentous decisions for himself. He became aware of the network of relationships and responsibilities of his present life. The Rebbe helped the Hasid to bear the shock of sharing the experience of cosmic consciousness, of experiencing the complete and yet dynamic oneness of the All.

The Hasid knows the function of being helped, while the function of the Lord is to be the unmoved source of the energies. The function of the Rebbe is to be the one who re-members, who so polarizes the random divine energies that they will be at the service of the Hasid, and who so polarizes the Hasid that he will be at the service of God, as one polarizes waves of sound and light into music and color.

This encounter frequently came in a highly structured situation (not unlike the mondo of Zen). Sometimes it was necessary for the Rebbe to shock his Hasid into insight and enlightenment. However, there was always a great element of compassion on the part of the Rebbe.

> Once two children, the sons of Reb Shmuel of Lubavitch, were playing at the game of Rebbe and Hasid. Reb Zalman Ahron, then seven years old, was playing Rebbe, while his younger brother, Reb Shalom Dov Baer then five years old, played Hasid. The younger brother girded his loins with a prayer sash, knocked softly at the door, and when invited to enter, approached his brother on tiptoe and said "Master, please give me a tikkun [healing prescription] for my soul."
>
> "What have you done?" the elder brother demanded.
>
> "I have stolen a pickle from Mother." At this point Reb Zalman Ahron laughed, whereupon Reb Shalom Dov Baer, frustrated, turned to his older brother and said, "You are not a rebbe. A rebbe never laughs at the distress of a Hasid."
>
> Another time the two brothers were playing the same game in the same positions. Reb Shalom Dov Baer asked for a tikkun for not having recited the blessing after eating an apple. Reb Zalman Ahron replied: "For the next forty days you

> are to recite a blessing out of the prayer manual after eating any food."
>
> "You did not do it right," his younger brother reproached him.
>
> "How can you say this," Reb Zalman Ahron argued, "I myself watched Daddy through the keyhole when a Hasid asked him the very same question, and I gave you his exact reply."
>
> "I too watched Daddy," Reb Shalom Dov Baer replied, "but you don't do it right. Daddy always sighs before he answers."

To the Hasid, and this is still the practice today, all matters fell properly under the guidance of the Rebbe. The Hasid, considering a minor matter, shrugs his shoulders and says: "Who is to know what is major and what is minor? Matter, spirit, soul, Torah—in all of these, one must unify His Blessed Name. The consequences of a single seemingly unimportant step may involve one's entire life or lives."

Many seekers have found their way to the Rebbes of our day. At Lubavitch, Satmar, and Bobov in Brooklyn, at Belz and Ger in Israel, among numerous others, modern baal teshuvahs—returnees to Judaism and Hasidism—have found their place. The transformations they undergo in the process of *teshuvah* (return, or repentance) is for them ample evidence of the spiritual potency of Hasidism.

There are others, having awakened their consciousness in the Aquarian headspace, who see in Hasidism a way to discover the Rebbe in themselves and in each other. In Neo-Hasidic celebrations, they often preside together in a nonhierarchical manner, or in turn as the spirit manifests itself in their midst.

The Aquarian Minyan in Berkeley, California is a clear example, at present, of such an association. There are also other growth and gestalt groups (notably Chrysalis in Boston) that utilize various Hasidic techniques of spiritual direction and communal devotion.

To help others in the Aquarian headspace find their bearings in the inner world of the Kabbalah, we move to the next chapter.

NOTES

1 Elijah De Vidas (1518–1587) was a sixteenth-century Kabbalistic writer and author of the spiritual guide book *Reishit Chokhmah.*

2 Isaac Luria (1534–1572), also known as the Holy Ari (lion) and the Arizal, was a mystic who left a great impression on many aspects of Jewish thought and prayer. He lived in Safed, in the Holy Land, where a school of Kabbalah formed around him and Moses Cordovero (d. 1570). Chaim Vital (1543–1620) was the chief disciple of the Holy Ari, and compiled his master's teachings in a book called the *Etz Hayim* (The Tree of Life). This circle of Safed Kabbalists changed and broadened Jewish mysticism dramatically in an attempt to revitalize the spiritual life of the Jewish people and of all humanity by infusing all religious practices with deep spiritual consciousness.

To Walk in Paradise: An Introduction to Kabbalah

If our book were a historic, definitive text on the Kabbalah, we might have begun by defining our topic as the chain of inner transmission of the secrets of Jewish esotericism. We would have given names, dates, and places, all of which are available in excellent articles on the subject in the new *Encyclopedia Judaica* by Professor Gershom G. Scholem. But our text is an introduction into the *process* of Kabbalah. We therefore want to meet you and the subject of Kabbalah in a different space.

Even when we just realize that there are different mental and spiritual spaces, we are already engaged in some form of the Kabbalah. When we name them, we are in the realm of Worlds and *Sefirot* (divine emanations and attributes of God). When we find ways to describe how to get in touch with these spaces in us and in the cosmos, and in actuality bring about contact with them, effecting changes in our lives, we are involved in the practical aspect of the Kabbalah.

When we enter into meditation and are in touch with the inner vision, observing the dynamics of the interaction of names, worlds, and Sefirot in us, we see through the speculum: we are involved in speculative Kabbalah. Yet Kabbalah, as a system, can also be helpful in providing us with a vocabulary of the inner and higher life. So it pays to learn its language, especially because it allows us to hear what sage, seer, and saint observed and transmitted to us.

Kabbalists come in many varieties. Each one will, of course, claim to be the real Kabbalist and all others mere facsimiles, less genuine than himself. In order that we might identify them and hear their voices, let us discuss three main types, indicating their characters, major modes of function, and the playing fields of consciousness with which they concern themselves.

The Fundamentalist Kabbalist

The fundamentalist Kabbalist speaks with a stern authoritative voice. He has fulfilled the orthodox legal requirements of "filling his belly with Talmud and codes." He is over forty years old, meticulous in his observance of the most specific details of halacha, and of exemplary virtue, having completed all the penances for the sins of his youth. Requirements for him are those spelled out by Rabbi Chaim Vital in his *Gate to Holiness*, part of which can be found in the third section of this book. He would consider all other "Kabbalists" not only charlatans, but also dangerous—capable of misleading others and causing damage in the cosmos and to themselves. His major mode of function is in Torah. Not satisfied by the study of it only on the levels of *peshat* (contextual), *remez* (hint), *derash* (interpretation), he strives to penetrate into the level of *sod*—of mystery. To do so, the fundamentalist Kabbalist employs such means as gematria, *notarikon*, *hilluf*, and *temurah*. These tools can be described briefly.

Gematria: Gematria is the system in which the equal numerical value of otherwise dissimilar words and phrases are plumbed for hidden meanings and correspondences. For example, the sages say, "Enters the wine, exits the secret." They came to this conclusion because the values of the Hebrew words *yayin* (wine) and sod (secret) both equal seventy, meaning the numerical value of the individual letters, when added up, is seventy for both words. The Kabbalist therefore concludes that the differences between "wine" and "secret" are only variations of form and not of essential quantity on a spiritual level. This change in form is what constitutes for the human mind a change in quality and substance. Yet the total number of vibrations energizing both remains constant.

Notarikon: Notarikon is a system that breaks words into sentences composed of their initial letters. The first word of the Ten Commandments, for example, *anochi*, meaning "I am," hints at the sentence "*Ana nafshi katavit yahavit*," which means "I have written and given myself to you in this book." From this, the Kabbalist derives the meaning that God's presence becomes manifested in the written Torah and that studying it is a means of communion.

Hilluf and Temurah: This system allows the Kabbalist to change the sequence of a word's letters in order to change realities from malign to benign value. The word *nega*, for example, meaning "plague," can be turned into *oneg*, meaning "delight." The Kabbalist may also use a process of prayer and contemplation in which each instance of the Divine Four-Letter Name (although pronounced *adonai)* is visualized in the context of the *Sefirah*, or divine attribute, being expressed by the Tetragrammaton, YHVH, and punctuated by the vowels associated with that particular Sefirah, for example, *YoHo VoHo*.

Other techniques include attempts to bring about *yichud* (unification) or *shiluv* (interspersing). He would visualize, for example, the letters of YHVH and adonai (ADNY) together as *YAHDVNHY* or *AYDHNVYH*. The idea is that by creating new names, the Kabbalist sets up new channels for the flow of the Divine Life and Light to enter the world.

This Kabbalist mainly concerns himself with seeking the hidden meaning *(nistar)* of Torah in the manifest meaning *(nigleh)*.

By and large, the fundamentalist has received his training from other Kabbalists who preceded him and whose learning from tradition and books have been validated by experiences of *ru'ach hakodesh* or *gillui Eliyahu* (the "Revelation of Elijah," that is, encountering the prophets either in the flesh or in one's consciousness). Trusting the teacher's spiritual validation, this Kabbalist follows his teacher's direction until he himself merits such validation by the grace of God.

In Orthodox Hasidism, this process still continues for the most part, except that the teachings and interpretations of the Rebbe serve the devotee as the main text for study and contemplation. In the Hasidic version of fundamentalist Kabbalah, the use of combining Divine Names for achieving unification (as well as other goals) has fallen into disuse; its place has been taken by techniques to achieve states of feeling, such as love, fervor, awe, and faith.

The very idea of the fundamentalist Kabbalist seems to us today to be a contradiction in terms. Kabbalah, which seeks to free itself from the fetters of constrictive, mundane, denotative thinking, does not seem to lend itself to fundamentalism. Furthermore, the fundamentalist Kabbalist, who cuts himself off by choice (reinforced by communal peer pressure) from contemporary thought and experience, cannot be in touch with what the Holy Spirit reveals in this generation. He also finds himself in a conflict he cannot easily resolve. The same forces that cut him off from contemporary thought and experience also sever him from the acceptance of other religions as vehicles for the transmission of Divine Life and Light. Reb Nachman of Breslov, who dared to profess that "the Holy Spirit shouts forth even from the tales of the gentiles," found himself under heavy fire for his daring in this and other matters. Yet the perennial philosophy in which the Divine Light and Life transcends the limits of creed and dogma is part of our intuition. The fundamentalist Kabbalist cannot resolve this dilemma and still remain true to his exclusivist tradition.

Characteristically, the fundamentalist Kabbalist is heavy. He enters into his consciousness as if it were the only one describing this and other realities. It is largely static. His worlds do not dance freely. He would be disturbed to think of his involvement in the mysteries as a cosmic game or dance.

Involved in a cosmic battle between the forces of holiness and klippot (shells, the forces of evil), he is solemn and serious and not much in touch with his own body. Only the paradigmatic complete tzadik can afford to do that! For the tzadik, every carnal thought leads to God. But most fundamentalist Kabbalists are warned to refrain from such risky attempts and are bidden to suppress such thoughts. For them, the time has not yet arrived (prior to the Messiah) when the Torah is engraved in their own limbs. Yet great *tzadikim*, like the Baal Shem Tov, are in touch not only with heaven, but also grounded in their body, and even were known to understand body-language and the language of plants and animals. Because the fundamentalist Kabbalist is so wary of carnality, he only can trust the guidelines of the Law in its strictest observance.

What follows now are typical admonitions, warning the fundamentalist Kabbalist that none of the comparisons he will find in his studies should be mistaken to refer to the physical level. This selection is composed from several tracts and commentaries, translated and brought together to give the flavor of fundamentalist Kabbalah texts:

> Know that in order to help one understand, permission was granted to utilize the limbs of the body as a simile, as it is written: "From my flesh do I see God" (Job 19:26). Yet you, in your wisdom, purify your thought to know that in the highest realms, there is nothing physical, far be it. Anything that happens higher than the *atzilut*, we have no permission to deal with, nor to compare it with anything that has form and likeness. It is only a means to explain things to the ear. Thus we utilize a simile. Yet he who is wise understands from his experience that no form exists there at all. However, from the Ten Sefirot downward, we have permission to talk in simile and likeness.
>
> Do not let your thoughts seduce you to say that on the *atzilic* plane there are visible forms and colors. Those who assume such are called to the nether-world and judged for having assigned thing-like dimensions to the Lord of Lords! In such dimensions there is no color or form. He who is exalted even over the highest sees and is not visible. Yet in truth, it is also true that form and color originate from there. But they do not manifest except as they emanate downward. Having descended and fallen from the high place where they are rooted, they issue forth in colors.
>
> And when you see terms like "male," "female," "mating," and

"kisses," you ought to know that by "male" is meant the Sefirot which give the energy to the one who receives it, which we call "female." Thus the mystery of the "mating" which is attributed to the Sefirot is the connecting and the cleaving of the "male," which issues the energies unto the "female," which in union receives them. In this sense are the hard rigors of the "female" sweetened by the graces of the "male."

So, too, in the creation of the world, when the mode of judgment was merged with the mode of compassion, this itself was in the mystery of the "mating" and "kissing." In this sense, spirit cleaves to spirit in the spirituality of the Sefirot. And what is meant by the mystery of "pregnancy"? The "female" receives from the "male" the root of what is to become, and fixes that in the spirit. When this is yet in the "male," it exists there in a subtle yet undefined manner. In the "female," it is developed to assume manifest existence in actuality. So we read in the Zohar: "They [the Sefirot] are all contained in *chokhmah.* From there they issue only on specific paths to *binah,* where they become fixed. This then is what scripture means by: *And by understanding* [binah] *do the heavens become established* (Prov. 3 19). All of them You made by chokhmah in binah."

The mystery of "birth" and "nurturing" refers to the evolving of existing beings from their subtle beginnings to concrete existence and fulfillment.

Know therefore that the wise ones of the Zohar and the Ari of blessed memory [Isaac Luria] needed to utilize these terms and descriptions borrowed from the body repertoire in order to clarify such mysteries, which otherwise could not be expressed except by means of such terms and physical analogues. Permission was granted to utilize analogues of physical-bodythings in order to further understanding. This is so because the countenance of man is so amazingly made and ordered in the silhouette of Supernal Beings. This is all total spirituality and has nothing to do with physical light like that of a candle or that of the sun—far be it!

We are permitted to use the word *light* in speaking of the Divine and the spiritual because it refers to the most subtle of all senses—the most precious. Thus we may by simile alone make use of this term.

One born of woman cannot attain to these Sefirot. Even the Sefirot themselves cannot comprehend the light of the Sefirot that transcends them. How much more so the Eyn Sof that gives them all life! It cannot be limited by comprehension. So how can a person even begin to comprehend the Eyn Sof?

When we conceive of these things, it is not they whom we know, but their effects on our scale of observation. We do not therefore know the Sefirot themselves, nor their power which the Eyn Sof has invested in them to conduct the affairs of those here below.

You may ask, what is the point of attempting to climb this dangerous mountain of the Lord? Is it not better to be satisfied studying the manifest, simpler parts of the Torah? The answer is that each serious "Disciple of the Wise" has the obligation, if he recognizes his Creator, to know Him. This wisdom consists of several basic questions. First, one needs to know oneself. Who am I? How was I created? Where do I come from and where am I going? How is the body formed to function? How must I give an account of myself before the Ruler of All?

Another question deals with the secret of the soul. What is the soul within me? Where does it come from? Why did it come to this body, which is made from a drop of semen?

> Another dimension is to discover and contemplate the mystery of the Divine Master. All these things one can reach in truly understanding the mysteries of Torah. Through the wisdom of Kabbalah, one may understand the mystery of oneness and the arcana of divine conduct. By a hint, one may learn how the limbs, attributes, and names which are written in the Torah refer to the Creator; how they are unified and "mated" through the Torah and the Commandments. One may learn of the rungs of the souls and the angels, what heaven and hell are about, what the klippot are, and the sparks they contain, which need to be freed so they can be returned to their holy source. So, Rabbi Chaim Vital states that the entire intent in our teshuvah [the turning or re-turning to God, or to our selves] and good works is to draw down the divine influence called *yosher* into the ordered universe. The 613 Commandments mirror the 613 veins and limbs of God. Thus can a person reach fulfillment in the mysteries of Torah and find grace and life in the eyes of God and man.

The chapters included in the third section of this book, excerpts from *Gates of Holiness* and *Patach Eliyahu*, are further examples of traditional Kabbalistic texts.

The Behaviorist Historian of Kabbalistic Studies

There is another possible way to view the history and development of Kabbalah. This is the way of the behaviorist historian. Instead of viewing the Kabbalah specifically as divinely revealed Torah, he sees in it the empirical accumulation of the doctrines concerning the inner way; neither more nor less important than the accumulated wisdom that leads to the construction and operation of automobiles. One is a vehicle for the body, the other is a vehicle for a flight of consciousness. Given that a person has taken care of the needs of his biological maintenance and wishes to indulge in such flights of consciousness, the way of Kabbalah is as good, and as imperfect, as the ways of yoga, Zen, or drugs.

Empirical knowledge is accumulated by people who have learned from natural existence that which is useful to them. In this way, they have transmitted to others the knowledge that they have gained through trial and error. Ultimately, however, this person may judge that such flights of consciousness are a pastime and a luxury.

If the behaviorist also possesses a sense of humor, he might see the pursuit of consciousness as a form of aesthetic and philosophical entertainment. Structuring such entertainment according to game rules and payoffs, he might even come to respect the Kabbalistic enterprise as some sort of multidimensional chess, in which the adepts pursue their pleasure. The universe for him, however, is generally neutral and ultimately purposeless. In view of this, as long as the adept realizes that he and his fellows are playing a game, the behaviorist historian of the Kabbalah has no objections. He will, however, object vigorously to the adept involving *him* in this game (unless he is provided with an exit that will leave the game behind). The well-informed student of Kabbalah who is in the position of the behaviorist historian may very well be able to teach us a great deal of the Kabbalah and its history. He might delineate for us the development of concepts to the point that we would understand them even better than if we were to study at the feet of a fundamentalist Kabbalist.

He could be a more effective teacher than the fundamentalist because he would organize the material, concepts, and content in the same coherent manner that would more closely correspond to the way in which our minds have been regimented from our first year in school. While the behaviorist teaches in a familiar Western way, the fundamentalist teaches from a dense, closed web of interlacing Torah homilies that seem to have no clear beginning and no clear end. Instead of leading us from axiom to conclusion via ordered and progressive corollaries, the fundamentalist leads us down circuitous paths, and seems to get lost in finesses unrelated to one another, mixing puns and gematria into a mélange of ideas. Worse yet, in the case of Lurianic materials, a kind of algebraic calculus is invented as a form of shorthand, which in no one place is made explicit. We might well yearn for the clear and schematic exposition of Lurianic materials of the behaviorist historian of the Kabbalah.

What remains essential for the Aquarian seeker is to find in this jungle-like garden of exotic medicinalia a healing for his own yearning and dis-ease. He will not be helped by either the traditional fundamentalist Kabbalist, or the behaviorist historian of Kabbalah studies. The first does not recognize the Aquarian's condition as valid. His advice to that seeker would be to become an anachronism, to close himself off from the universal stream of global communication (or at least a large part of it) and from the spirit of the times. In fact, many who have for a time taken up residence in the camp of the fundamentalist type of Kabbalist have had to leave that nostalgic place when they felt that their specific needs have not been met. It is not probable that the behaviorist historian of the Kabbalah can help him either, for his approach lacks access to the transcendental realm in the here-and-now that many of us so urgently desire. Lacking models in the past, the New Age seeker must forge his own. Through this process he rediscovers the Kabbalah and learns to use it to help him on his path.

The Humanistic Transcendentalist of the Kabbalah

The humanistic transcendentalist wants to achieve the highest level of religious intensity without feeling compelled to develop fanaticism at the same time. True, all the evidence of the past points to their inseparability. Yet the working hypothesis of our humanist is that not only is religious depth without fanaticism desirable, but that it *must* be achieved. He therefore seeks, among other things, to enter into a dialogue of devoutness with seekers of other faiths, comparing ways, techniques, and methods for how to focus awareness of God, how to make prayer life more relevant and effective, and how to become a clearer and better channel for the infinite light of creation.

He is a humanist because the enterprise of human beings contacting the Cosmic Mind is of great concern to him. He realizes that all revelation is as much a function of the revealer as it is the function of the seeker. The Divine Revealer depends on man for the piano keys on which to play His revelation. The content of the symphony, the revelation, is limited by the range of the instrument: the consciousness of the seeker's mind. The phenomena that psychology discusses under the categories of set and setting determine the focus, the scale of observation, the depth of field, as well as the sensitivity of the human instrument.

This humanism is not new to Torah. The sages referred to it in terms of the Torah speaking in the language of man. Our humanist knows, however, that even the conditions of his set, setting, sensitivity, and so on are the results of the unfolding of the divine plan. He does not cut himself off from the Divine Immanence that produced him in the here-and-now. As he participates in the process of revelation (a mutuality akin to lovemaking), his contribution to the process is no less important and ecstasy-producing than that of his divine partner. (For this reason Kabbalists even of the fundamentalist variety speak of this dialogue as the conjunction of male and female, and so every act is one of unification between the Holy One, blessed be He, and the divine feminine aspect Shekhinah.) Still he makes an act of faith and unification, recognizing that on the monistic level even his own contribution is divine. For this reason we think of him not only as humanistic, but also as transcendentalist.

He is a Kabbalist because he respects the process in which not only his mind, but also those of all his predecessors, interact with God. In studying their interactions with the Divine, he is no less turned on than the lover who sets his own inner stage by reading erotic literature. Looking at Shimon Bar Yochai of the Zohar, Abraham Abulafia, Moses Cordovero, Isaac Luria, and the Hasidic masters, our humanistic Kabbalist is prepared to receive the divine influx in himself. This, for him, is of supreme value. He immerses himself in the literature to the extent of his ability, in the original if he is capable, or in what is available in translation if not. And because he is a humanist, he immerses himself not only in Jewish sources, but also in those coming from other traditions which arouse him to greater receptivity of the cosmic.

Humanistic psychology, as well as its closely allied neighbor, transpersonal psychology, are for him arsenals of psychic tools. Gestalt, from its first academic figure-ground application to its therapeutic intrapersonal flips, allows him to change places with God in his inner life. (The chapter "Finnegan's Awakening" is a move-by-move simulation of this process.)

Carnality is no threat to the humanist. Having resensitized himself, often at great personal cost in therapy, he has managed to set aside some of the sabotage that society and the school system have inflicted upon him. When he tastes food, or becomes aware of a fragrance, or enjoys the harmonies of sight and sound, or the tender feeling generated by touch, he may actually be saying "Thank God!" more than the hundred times per day that the Law requires blessings to be recited. He is moved to profound meditation on the Sefirot when giving or receiving a massage. Massaging the right arm and right section of the chest and back, he can contact, in his consciousness, the divine attribute of *chesed,* and thus can follow the tree of the Sefirot over the entire body. When we ask him how he construes this "holy carnality," he might respond by explicating Scripture:

> *Umevasari echzeh Elohah.* "From my flesh I see God." The verb used here is not *ereh,* "I shall see clearly or objectively," but *echzeh,* a verb used to denote inner vision, prophecy. The Divine Name *Elohah* is not the name of any particular attribute, but the undifferentiated God available to vision through my body. From my right hand, I can envision *El* (the Kind One, chesed). From my heart, I can envision YHVH (the indescribably Beautiful One, *tiferet),* and so forth, through the various parts of the body.

> When my body is in the right tone, alive, aware, and tingling, such vision becomes possible. I am in touch with my vehicle and I can visualize the Divine, being in touch with His Name. When I am aware of my breath—breathing in—I am in touch with *neshamah* (my soul) and the world of *beriyah* (creation) and the world of *yetzirah* (formation), and when I breath out I'm in touch with *nefesh* (animation) and the world of *asiyah* (function).
>
> To put it differently: When I am in my head, I am in the letter *yud* of the Divine Name YHVH and in the world of atzilut. When I am in my chest and arms and aware of my breath, I am in the letter *heh*, a breath letter, and in beriyah. When I'm in my spine going from the base to the top, I am in the letter *vav* and the world of yetzirah, and when I am in my legs and pelvis, I am in the letter heh, the final letter in the Name and in the world of asiyah.
>
> In becoming aware of these significances, I begin to realize that the body is not only the Temple of the spirit, but it is my special altar to God to serve Him when tasting and feeling. I can, thereby, give back to Him the gift of my particular sensations.

The humanist's carnality is integrated with his spirituality.

What then is *our* bias? We want all the benefits to our interior life that we can gain from as close an identification as we can manage with the fundamentalist Kabbalist. We will, for the sake of entering into the tryst of consciousness with God, suspend our critical disbelief. Somewhere in the back of our minds we will also hold onto the rich storehouse of information concerning historical data and content of the Kabbalah that we have received from the behaviorist historian of Kabbalah. But most of all, we are committed to be in the here-and-now with an eye to move the center to the periphery, and the periphery to the center, thus turning the here into everywhere, and the now into the eternal present.

What are our tools? In communicating with one another, we

often face the problem of not meeting in the same universe of discourse. The nomenclature of the Kabbalah provides us with a roadmap of consciousness. For the Kabbalist, to indicate a space is to give a very precise address to a consciousness-meeting place—for example, as Luria does in a discussion on the "the ru'ach of tiferet of yetzirah." What is being said about this space, of course, is dependent upon the context. In Luria's discussion, yetzirah refers to one of the Kabbalistic worlds, ru'ach refers to one of the levels of the soul, and tiferet refers to one of the Sefirot. Thus, when we impose our construct-grid on the totality of being, it has as much reality as, for example, longitude and latitude found only on maps and never in reality, nevertheless indicating a meeting place for two people who want to find one another.

What do we mean by "worlds"? In the language of the Kabbalists, we are talking about higher worlds and lower worlds. "High" and "low" are conveniences, habits of language acquired over a long time. We only borrow these terms and they will continue to sound as if special dimensions are meant, but it is not necessary to remind the reader that where inner spaces are concerned, "low" and "high" intermingle on our plane of reality just like low and high frequencies in the range of radio waves. God-realization, however, is possible in any one of those worlds, high or low. In the pages below, the reader will find two charts that lay out this nomenclature.

The world of physical reality is known as "physical asiyah." In it, we do the kind of work for which we have to be paid. We have no emotional investment in it one way or another. The seeker resides in this world with skillful equanimity. Looking at the chart of the worlds, we can see in the line for physical asiyah that it represents functions in the world of action. The electromagnetic spectrum of matter, waves, and particles represent the action and the actors. The physical body is grounded in this world. The elements of the earth and the mineral kingdom are ways of reflecting the substance of this world. It is the consciousness of the complete *rasha* (animalistic egoist) as portrayed in the *Tanya*. The Torah consciousness engendered in this world is mostly mechanical and deals with grammar and vocabulary.

As we proceed upward on the chart of the worlds, we now enter three spiritual universes, each one progressively "higher" than the last: spiritual asiyah, yetzirah, and beriyah. We now can follow the chart according to the different columns, each one indicating the hierarchy of that particular dimension. Following, for example, the aspects of the soul, where the physical body was located in physical asiyah, we find nefesh on the level of spiritual asiyah. In the Kabbalah, "soul" has several names, each one corresponding to a different aspect of soul. In yetzirah, we find ru'ach, and on the level of beriyah, we find neshamah. In the spiritual realm, we can go no higher than beriyah. Transcending, however, the *parsah,* the ego barrier, which no created object can pass, by opening the door of transcendence, we may be able to find ourselves taken up to the soul level of *chayah* in the world of atzilut and the level of *yechidah* in *Adam Kadmon.* Only the pure Eyn Sof transcends the contraction barrier of infinity which Kabbalists call *tzimtzum.*

Experientially, the world of spiritual asiyah is one where we perform the kind of function that requires no other reward outside of its own doing. Of this, the sages spoke when they said "the reward of the mitzvah is the mitzvah itself." On that level, the only intention that matters is that the devotee sees his function as doing God's will. The Sefirah of *malkhut* calls on him to accept the yoke of the Kingdom of Heaven. However, usually other motivations accompany the doing of a mitzvah. On the level of yetzirah and ru'ach, he also feels the influence of the seven Sefirot that charge him with the emotional energies of love and awe. They are derived from ru'ach and the six Sefirot from chesed to *yesod.* The consciousness of the world of yetzirah is that of the fervent devotee. However, even this motivation for doing a mitzvah is further charged by an intellectual motivation that derives from the world of beriyah. The soul aspect of neshamah is not satisfied by the emotions alone. Yearning for cosmic perspective, nothing less than the ability to perceive patterns connecting alpha to omega, with everything in between, satisfies him who worships God with his mind. He is the one who meditates at great length on the meaning of everything. He deals in signification and communicates with others in terms of integrated signification. In doing a mitzvah, neshamah rides on the general obedience to God of nefesh, on the emotional fervor of ru'ach, and further charges the act with the significance of thought. The neshamah lives in the world of beriyah. Beriyah is energized by the Sefirah of binah, which seeks to understand everything in detail and specificity. This understanding is very far from ego-heavy conceptualization. On the contrary, it participates with the *seraphim*, the angelic mind entities, in an egoless contemplation of God-in-the universe-and-history. While the neshamah finds fulfillment in this intellection, it yearns even further to transcend this sublime mentation and courts its own annihilation, seeking to transcend itself by manifesting its divine core, chayah and yechidah. A mitzvah done with the manifestation of chayah and yechidah is no longer doing someone else's will, but rather it is the divine will expressing itself through the vehicle of the now egoless devotee.

We have followed the devotee in their service of God through the chart. We now find that the chart and its details have become useful for us to isolate the different universes of discourse in which the Kabbalists can meet. The designations ru'ach and yetzirah are now meaningful coordinates. We now turn to another chart dealing with the Sefirot from which the term tiferet comes to us.

The chart of the Sefirot is a schematization of material found throughout the Zohar and epitomized in *Patach Eliyahu* (see later chapter). Our categories in this chart are the days of creation, parts of the body, names of the Sefirot, archetypal personalities, names and aspects of God, and finally, referring back to the chart of the worlds, levels of consciousness manifest in the various worlds. We now locate tiferet on our chart under the heading Sefirot. Tiferet is also known as *rachamim*. Tiferet means "beauty," and rachamim means "compassion," derived from the root *rechem*, "womb." The feeling tone of tiferet is manifested in the third day of creation in which God twice said, "It is good." Relating to the body, it represents the thoracic cavity, the region of the heart. The Divine Name reflecting the light of tiferet *is* the Tetragrammaton in its lower manifestation. In its higher manifestation, this name sometimes alludes to the Thirteen Attributes of Mercy, which blossom forth in *keter* and energize the Yom Kippur experience. Archetypically, Jacob/Israel, the third patriarch, manifests tiferet in a male physical body. In the feminine manifestation, Chana, the mother of the prophet Samuel, can be seen as its personification. The awareness of yetzirah is energized by the three Sefirot of chesed, *gevurah*, and tiferet, with tiferet being the heart of yetzirah. Tiferet is most alive and radiant when connected to keter. It transmits the energy of keter via yesod to the recipient malkhut. Tiferet thus is referred to as "Jacob's Ladder," and the vav of the Divine Name.

The Kabbalistic humanist equips people active in the Aquarian Age with a map of the inner spaces, opens to them access to not only the mysticism of the Far East, but also the mysticism, Jewish and Christian, of the Western tradition. As significator and integrator, a person possessed of the Aquarian consciousness will soon enough find equivalences and transformations on his own. He will recognize the world of asiyah as that of the karma yogi, for example; the world of yetzirah as that of the bhakti yogi, and so on. Syncretic connections such as *Shiva-gevurah, Vishnu-chesed,* and *Brahma-tiferet* will jump into his awareness.

> Shmuel Munkes was on his way to the rebbe. On foot of course, like the song says, "to the rebbe you walk like a pilgrim...to the rebbe you don't ride," his bag over his shoulders, a song on his lips, and thoughts containing universes in his head.
>
> Clippetty-clop, a carriage comes down the road. In it sits a dandy, dressed in pretense. The carriage stops and a voice says to Shmuel, "Where to, young man?"
>
> "To Lyozhna, to my rebbe,"
>
> "What coincidence! I too am traveling to him. Come share the ride and tell me about him."
>
> "And who are you?" asks Shmuel, now seated beside the dandy.
>
> "I am a Kabbalist," says he, "the son and grandson of Kabbalists. You see," pointed the dandy to his head, "my grandfather was into the Kabbalah up to here, my father was

into Kabbalah up to the navel, and I," said he as he pointed to his knees, "up to here. I heard that this Rebbe Shneur Zalman is also into the Kabbalah so I want to get to know him and test if he knows anything at all."

"Wow," said Reb Shmuel, "you mean you are a Kabbalist? Maybe you can help me with a text."

"A text?"

"Yes—you see, I studied Luria's *Tree of Life* and in the book I found a scrap with this holy statement, so cosmic and so puzzling; maybe you can tell me what it means."

"Tell me what did it say?"

"It said:

> 'In the very primal beginning
> There was chaos—all was sundered
> and separate. Grainy nuclei unconnected.
> Swirling. Then flat, they were in one sphere.
> The sphere unfolded into an orb. On the orb, lines
> appeared. Forces cut the space into fields.
> These fields became centered in a point and
> enfolded the point.
> Peace was made between the fiery angels
> and the angels of the vital fluid
> and in their cooperation all came out
> as it ought to be.'"

"What an amazing text! How authentic to the Kabbalah! Is it Zoharic? No—Cordovarian? No—Lurianic? No—post-Lurianic? No—it has too ancient a ring for that. What an amazing text. No, I cannot place it."

Says Shmuel, "Well, you see, I am only a young snip of a Hasid and will have to wait weeks before they let me see the rebbe. And you, a Kabbalist up to the knees, the son of a Kabbalist up to the navel, and the grandson of a Kabbalist up to the forehead, you who travel in the 'chariot' will get to see him pretty soon after you arrive in Lyozhna. So do ask him and tell me too what he says."

"Sure enough my young friend; let's recite the text again."

"In the very primal beginning..." they chant in unison.

He does not have long to wait, the dandy Kabbalist up-to-his-knees. They let him in to see the rebbe, and after he introduces himself, he proposes the text heard from the young Shmuel:

"In the very primal beginning..."

The rebbe closes his eyes and stares into the inner places, he tries to see the text as a reality. He searches from alpha to omega and, yes, the text makes sense. It means something, and he opens his eyes and turns to the dandy: It is just kreplach (a ravioli)!

In the very primal beginning
There was chaos—all was sundered
and separate, grainy nuclei unconnected
Swirling.
  (That was the flour.)
Then flat, they were in one sphere.
  (The flour became dough.)
The sphere unfolded into an orb.
  (The dough was rolled out flat.)
On the orb, lines appeared.
Forces cut the space into fields.
  (Of course—diamond shaped pieces of dough were cut and meat was put in.)
These fields became centered in a point and
enfolded the point.
Peace was made between the fiery angels
and the angels of the vital fluid.
  (As the pot was filled with water and put on the stove to boil, the kreplach were put in.)
And in their cooperation all came out as it ought to be!

> I guess the dandy learned what Kabbalah is all about. The rebbe laughed when he finally saw Shmuel. "What a dish you cooked up," he said.

Now why did I tell you the story? You still don't understand? Oy! What am I going to do with you! How can I teach you *Chasidus* and Kabbalah if you still don't see the point? How did the rebbe hear a text? It has to be something real. This text did not make any sense

Chart of the Worlds

Cosmic awareness / world	Which Sefirah is active	Torah perception (level of holy scripture)	Type of energy	Soul aspect
the no-thing • Eyn Sof absolute • beyond all worlds • tzimtzum • contraction • creation				
Adam Kadmon (First Man)	Keter (crown)	Ineffable	*Atik*, Keter, *Arikh*	Yechidah (the unique single One)
Atzilut (emanation)	Chokhmah (divine wisdom)	Sod (comprehension of the mystery)	All Sefirot present	Chayah (the Living One)
parsah • ego barrier • no object of creation can pass • transcendence door				
Beriyah (creation)	Binah	Derash (search); inductive awareness	Seraphim (angelic energy of thought)	Neshamah
Yetzirah (formation)	Sefirot	Remez (hint); deductive awareness	*Chayot* (chariot animals)	Ru'ach (spirit of man)
Asiyah (function)	Malkhut	Peshat (divested); simple meaning	*Ofanim* (wheels)	Nefesh
Physical asiyah (function in the world of action)		Grammar (mechanics)	Electromagnetic spectrum of matter	Physical bodies

on any other level, and this is also the way Shmuel constructed the "text." If you study Chasidus and Kabbalah and you hear words, visualize! See what real experience the words refer to, and if they are only words don't accept them; ask your *mashpi'ah* (Chasidus teacher) to give you an exercise so you might find out what the words mean. Make sure you understand Kabbalah and Chasidus on the level of kreplach!

Corresponding part of the Divine Name	**Active element**	**Realm**	**Faculty in use**	**Gurdjieff-Lilly space**
Top tip of yud	Quintessence beyond elements	Ideal of God	Delight; will; desire	1
Head of yud	Fire	Human ideal	Divine intellect	3
First heh	Air	Animal ideal	Thought	6
Vav	Water	Plant ideal	Feeling; speech; song	12
Last heh	Earth	Mineral ideal	Action	24
In the name	Earth	Mineral	Action	48

Chart of the Sefirot

Sefirot	Attributes of God	Day of creation	Male and female archetypes	Aspects of God
Keter (crown)	All-illuminating enlightenment	[Before creation]	[Beyond name and form]	*Ehyeh* (I Am)
Chokhmah	Divine wisdom; *abba* (father)	[Before creation]	[Beyond name and form]	*Asher* (That)
Binah	Divine understanding; *imma* (mother)	[Before creation]	[Beyond name and form]	Ehyeh (I Am)
Chesed	Loving-kindness; grace; *gedulah* (expansiveness)	1st day (Sunday)	Abraham; Miriam	El
Gevurah	Justice; rigor; *din* (judgment)	2nd day (Monday)	Isaac; Leah	*Elohim*
Tiferet	Beauty; mercy; rachamim (compassion)	3rd day (Tuesday)	Jacob; Hannah	YHVH
Netzach	Victory; eternity	4th day (Wednesday)	Moses; Rebecca	*Shaddai*
Hod	Glory	5th day (Thursday)	Aaron; Sarah	*Tzeva'ot*
Yesod	Foundation	6th day (Friday)	Joseph; Tamar	*Yah*
Malkhut	Majesty; kingdom	7th day (Shabbat)	David; Rachel	Adonai

Body parts of Universal One	Cosmic awareness
Crown of the head	Adam Kadmon (First Man)
Right brain	Atzilut (emanation)
Left brain	Beriyah (creation)
Right arm	Yetzirah (formation)
Left arm	Yetzirah (formation)
Heart area	Yetzirah (formation)
Right pelvis, kidney, thigh, ovary/testicle	Spiritual asiyah (function)
Left pelvis, kidney, thigh, ovary/testicle	Spiritual asiyah (function)
Male genitals; tongue	Spiritual asiyah (function)
Female genitals; mouth	Physical asiyah (function in action)

Remember the Sabbath

Somewhere between bondage and freedom, the Way is shown to each of us. The Sabbath is a real time-space-place to find that Way. It is a weekly retreat to that inside place where we get in touch with our higher mind, center our psyche, and find the next move in our lives.

The holy scriptures of all traditions are maps to enlightenment. The Torah tells how the children of Israel[1] were taken out of Egypt, across the Red Sea, and brought to Mount Sinai, where they received the Ten Commandments. They remained in the wilderness for forty years, until their slave mentality died off and they could enter the higher consciousness of the Promised Land.

The Jewish tradition teaches that each generation should regard itself as personally having left Egypt. What can each of us learn in our own personal spiritual journeys from this story?

The word *Torah* means "teaching." The name *Israel* means "God-wrestler," one who strives with the Divine, the spiritual seeker. Israel is the name Jacob the patriarch received after wrestling with the messenger of God. *Mitzraim*, the Hebrew name for Egypt, means "narrows," "ravine." Perhaps the ravines are the tight places in which we are caught seeking false gods such as our desires for fame, wealth, power, and sensory pleasures, which cannot fully satisfy our inner longings. After coming out of these ravines, each seeker may find a great water (of compassionate understanding) to cross, a spiritual mountain to ascend, and a continual encounter with God to maintain. We descend from these peak moments with a sense of having been given an assignment to effect changes in our daily lives. Just as a new generation was needed to enter the Promised Land, each of us needs patience to nurture our spiritual rebirths.

In the teachings of Torah, and in the Ten Commandments in particular, we have a road map to the Promised Land. The Fourth Commandment speaks of the seventh day:

> REMEMBER THE SEVENTH DAY TO HOLD IT SACRED. You are to labor and you must do all your work for six days. But the seventh day is a Sabbath to the Lord your God. You must not do any work, you nor your son nor your daughter, your slave man nor your slave girl, nor your domestic animal nor your temporary resident who is inside your gates. For in six days the Lord made the heavens and the earth, the seas and everything that is in them, and He proceeded to rest on the seventh day. That is why the Lord blessed the Sabbath day and proceeded to make it sacred. (Exodus 20:8–11)

These commandments are guidelines to find harmony with our fellow creatures, our environment, and our inner selves. Here, then, is a practical method of staying in touch with the Divine within. We are exhorted to remember the Sabbath day and hold it sacred.

Ordinary life on the Sabbath can be transformed into divine experience. For example, each meal can be an opportunity to learn, to sing, to serve, and to open up to the possibility of divine experience.

> Once the two holy brothers, Rabbi Elimelekh of Lizhensk and Rabbi Zushia of Annapol, went on a journey. They often traveled incognito, practicing *galut* (exile) and doing their thing to bring seekers and God together. After one particularly high Shabbos, after they had made havdalah (the ceremony at the end of Sabbath that marks its separation from other days), they turned to one another and said: "Do you suppose we really have reached so high that we have touched the source of

Shabbos in Heaven? Or is it perhaps that we have become adept at kidding ourselves? Maybe all that we have been doing is deceiving ourselves."

This question, by the way, is a terrifying one and there is no verbal answer one can give oneself. Maybe all that we do here is one fantastic collusion. Maybe there is really nothing transcendentally divine or even immanent in the whole spiritual business except that we are good at fooling ourselves and we have a good formula by which we do this.

At any rate, the two brothers decided to test the reality of their Shabbos. If they tried during the week and did not reach the higher realms, it would be a sign that it was for real, but if they would achieve Shabbos during the week, then it would prove that it was all a fake. So they set aside the next Wednesday, the very middle of the week, as their test Shabbos. All that they usually did on Friday to prepare for Shabbos, they did on Tuesday. They went to mikvah (ritual bath) and dressed in their Shabbos clothes and began to do the *Shir HaShirim* (The Song of Songs), chanting of their love for God and of His love for them and all Israel.[2]

"*Oh kiss me with the kisses of your mouth, for better is your lovemaking than wine*," then they recited *Mincha* (the afternoon prayer) and *Yedid Nefesh* ("The Soul's Friend"). *Quick lover, the time is coming, favor me with the taste of eternity.* Then came the whole "Friday night" unfolding—table hymns, Torah, Shabbos food, and all. The next morning and throughout the whole "Shabbos," they did not hold back a thing, but soared as they would on a very special Shabbos in flights of awareness that reached the highest heights.

After havdalah, they looked at each other and smiled a bitter smile. "Oy! What fakers we are! If we could do this on a Wednesday, then it is clear that we have just been kidding ourselves. What are we going to do?" And, as is befitting Hasidim when they have such problems, they went to their rebbe, the Maggid, to ask him.

As soon as they entered his study, he looked at them and said, "Tell me, dear brothers, where does the Shabbos go during the week?"

Perplexed, they could not answer. The rebbe looked at them, pointed his finger into the air, and said: "UP! That's where it goes! And when there are people like you who so deeply enter into the Shabbos as you did last Wednesday, the Shabbos comes down and dwells in you. You are holy, your service is holy, and the Holy One, Blessed be He, takes joy in you."

NOTES

1 All spiritual seekers of whatever faith or tradition who are "wrestling" with the creative energy in order to find themselves can be defined as "Israel."

2 In using the teachings translated from the masters of the past, we have something left of archaic forms of reverence intact. The fact that the Divine in Western culture is so often assigned the male pronoun, "He," may be misleading. According to the teachings of all major world religions, God is beyond form and sex, the essence of all life is beyond conceptual powers of the human mind. That divine and absolute essence, the Source of All, is surely beyond the duality of male/female definition. Nonetheless, we have left past language intact in this translation. These attitudes are changing now. Early authors spoke from a time, and group consciousness, which did assign gender to aspects of the Divine. Israel was "he," Torah and Sabbath were "she," and so on.

What Is Religion For?

There are two attitudes regarding the function of religion in the spiritual journey of the soul. The first sees all religious discipline as a vehicle to bring man to the great realization. As the Buddha would have it, the raft can be discarded after crossing the river. Or, as Ramakrishna[1] has said, the man travels to see the king in a carriage and with his retinue. But once he comes to the palace, he leaves everything outside and enters alone to meet the king.

The second attitude is illustrated by a story of the Maggid.[2] A man wears all sorts of travel clothes on the way to the capital and the palace of the king. Once he arrives, he takes out his best garment and dresses himself to see the king in his finest.

Though these two points of view are on one level diametrically opposed, both are of the opinion that all religion is but preparation for the moment of the truth in which the soul encounters God. The Far Eastern mode would have man discard discipline after discipline the closer he comes to the true union. It sees in the continuation of discipline a barrier, and after the encounter it is only so much excess baggage that is best discarded.

The Maggid's parable brings out the view that he who is farther away from the encounter can afford to have less discipline, but the closer one approaches the King, the more "court manners" one must display. "Those in His immediate environment must be meticulous as a hair's breadth," states the Midrash on Psalm 50:3. This Midrash tells how people who are still very far away do not have their actions scrutinized, but that the closer one gets to God, the more meticulous one needs to be in observance and holiness.

The redemptive process of the spiritual path works to redeem the soul from external and extraneous disciplines. The closer one comes, the less is needed from the outside. When one is raised to the rung of tzadik (righteous one, saint, spiritual master), there is only one precept left. "The tzadik shall live by his faith" (Hab. 2:4).

And yet, tzadikim who have been asked to describe how they shape their life in holiness describe their inner-faith-practice (in which they take all responsibility before God) in terms of the most detailed minutiae. This is not due to an obsession with details, but rather to a possession by God's presence in which everything is infinitely significant.

In any case, the experience of liberation, insight, and realization is seen as a result of the person's intense preparation for that moment that can, in some systems, be seen as a reward for intentional holiness, or in other systems, as a function of God's pure and underserved grace for which the saint has prepared fine and exquisite vessels to contain so great a gift.

There is still another function, perhaps more important, in the prescriptions of religion: guiding us back to the peak moment of realization. Consider the saint, the sage, the realized one who meets the moment when he both dies and is reconstituted by God's creative will and grace to be the person he was, in the same body and with the same basic qualities. He knows at this moment that as it was in the beginning, so it is now and forevermore. And yet, he will have to serve the Lord even from the point to which he has descended. So holy was the experience, and yet so fleeting, that at the moment he says YES to God—YES, I will work for the establishment of Your Kingdom; YES, I shall do and obey—at this very moment, an amnesia begins to set in, part of the vision is lost, and the saint knows that he will have to find all sorts of ways to re-member himself (to attach himself again to his Self). So he seeks out methods by which he can recall that most holy moment when he was in true touch with the sweet and holy grace, the brilliant and searing truth, the panoramic and infinite view of the Holy Land.

As he returns to the community with whom he shares his life, these reminders become part and parcel of the community's way of life, acting as windows to the infinite light.

The purpose of holy days is to reach certain aspects of that peak experience (which is itself in eternity, an all-at-onceness in the divine realm) as a community celebration. The upper and lower worlds are connected by a flow of energy. Holy days have been instituted by tzadikim (and what is the tradition but the transmission of generations of tzadikim?) to be a holy coming together of time, person, place, and word. The tzadik fully realizes that aspects of the holy moment can be reached at certain times in the cycle of life here below when he and the community celebrate this or that aspect of the divine realm.

In this manner, rituals, prescribed actions, thoughts, words, prayers, meditations, and books are ways to contact the higher realm. The father who circumcises his son is put in touch with God's will, with Abraham's experience, and with the experience of his own ancestors. There is immense power in the chain of experiences thus forged. A flowing together of cosmic dimensions occurs. Sparks of chaotic energy are freed from their randomness and redirected through the commandment, intention, and performance into the blessed realm of cosmic significance.

NOTES

1 Sri Ramakrishna (1836–1886) was an Indian yogi and saint.

2 The Maggid Dov Baer (1704–1772), preacher of Mezeritch, was a disciple and spiritual heir of the Baal Shem Tov.

Prayer

My Lord Creator of all,
Master of all worlds,
Supreme, compassionate, and forgiving,
Thank You for Your Torah,
Thank You for allowing me to learn from it
And to move toward serving You.
Thank You for revealing some of the
Mysteries of Your Way.
I'm amazed this is truly happening to me.

Please forgive my foolishness and unkindness,
The sins of my past.
Sincerely I pledge to live more uprightly
That I may be ever closer to You.
Fill me with that awe of You that opens my capacity
For loving.
And open my heart to the mysteries of Your Holy Way.
Reveal Your Torah, I pray.

I pray too that this study will bring You joy.
It is the incense I offer in Your Holy temple.
Bathe my soul, Your Soul, in the light
Of the source of all.

Lord, please remember, with me now, the kindness
And honesty of my ancestors who served You before.
Remember Your promise to care for the children
Of the righteous to the thousandth generation.
Enlighten me, if not for my own worth,
Then for theirs, and for the future growth of Your people.

Let Your radiance be recognized today, now,
In me and through me, that I may use the
Insights and energy of these, Your Holy
Teachings, for the good of all living creatures
Everywhere, and for the furtherance of
Your plan of the continuing creation.
Let no one anywhere be hurt by this study.
Guard my soul that stays on the straight
Path back to Your Home.

With King David, the joyful singer of Israel,
I pray "Open my eyes and let me see the
Wonders of Your Torah."
May the words of my mouth and the meditations
Of my heart find favor before You, O Lord,
My rock and my redeemer.

Based on the Hebrew text of a disciple of Isaac Luria

HASIDIC TRANSLATIONS

Introduction to Part Two

The road to the innermost aspect of Torah leads via the great minds of Kabbalah and Hasidism. Presumably one can penetrate the inner chambers directly, but then one would miss the apprenticeship. To learn from Rabbi Schneur Zalman[1] is to learn to stretch one's mind to the limit and to extend an idea to its own transcendence. To sit at the feet of Rebbe Nachman of Breslov is to learn how to connect thought and feeling clusters in unprecedented ways, and to make rabbit turns with the mind around words and meanings. Learn from Reb Ahrele Roth[2] how to live most energetically and devoutly in the midst of all the paradoxes of tradition.

Peak experience brings on amnesia; only that which was contained by the vessels of concepts acquired in the mind is retained. The more holy concepts one has, the more truth is rescued from oblivion. So, what I got from books I have found helpful. Indeed, some of what I learned in books so attracted my attention that I could not leave them after reading them in the original Hebrew or Yiddish. Because they initiated reverberations with my primary experience and thus brought the *forgotten* into the foreground consciousness, I felt compelled to translate and share them.

The test for inclusion in this book, then, was, "Did it re-turn me on?" If it did this for me *and* for others, it was included.

The best way to use these texts is to read them "out loud." This is close to a must. Torah reveals more to the ear—*Shema Yisrael!* Hear, Israel!—than to the eye. Only when the concepts have been made one's own do they group visually. Still, after reading the material, relax in your most comfortable meditation pose. Ask yourself, "What does this bring to mind?" Even if an idea at first repels you, ask yourself, "In what situation, under what circumstances, would this statement make sense and be true?" Then visualize the whole thing. Now make a devotional move, bringing your feeling to bear on the idea in such a way as to say to yourself, "This is not merely a mental exercise. This is reality, *my* own reality. This relates to my very own situation." As feeling begins to stir, gently fan this feeling by breathing it deeply into your lungs, sighing with it and letting the words of devoutness rise to your mouth. Chant the words over and over again. This whole thing you can offer as a gift to the Divine Self and with it, make a covenant with Spirit regarding the action-directive this idea has begotten in you.

There is still more to come. The task of rediscovering the Aquarian materials in Jewish mysticism has not even begun in a systematic way. But systematic is Piscean anyhow; and organic is Aquarian.

So share with me: "Eat, friends, drink, and be intoxicated lovers" (Song of Songs).

NOTES

1 Reb Shneur Zalman (1745–1813) of Liadi was the founder of Chabad Hasidism, also known as Lubavitch, and the author of the *Tanya*, a book of Hasidic teachings.

2 Reb Ahrele Roth (1894–1947) of Bergsas (Berehovo) and Jerusalem was a Hasidic rebbe, scholar, and author of the book *Shomer Emunim*.

A Ballad

A shtetl far from the highway,
Where the Jewish peasants
Do business with the neighboring village,
Work for the farmers.
In his room, door locked,
The rabbi studies,
And the books on his shelves multiply.

He makes his way to town,
Finds a holy book,
The seller names his price;
Weeks of wages! "I'll be back,"
And the rabbi goes to borrow the money.
In the morning, he is back, but
Too late; the bookseller cuts him off.
It's sold. Some coachman bought it
A coachman? A *baaleguleh*,[1] reading a book of Kabbalah?!

The rabbi, not knowing if the dealer teases,
Walks into the slum streets and asks for
The baalegulah who buys books.
They just stare at him. The last one on his list

Boards at the shoe-patcher's.
The rabbi gets his shoes patched.

He asks, "What's in these books you buy?"
"Oh," the baalegulah replies, "tales
and stories." The rabbi, his suspicions
Confirmed: "Could have guessed as much.
Imagine, baalegulahs and Kabbalah!"

His heart brined in salt, disgusted
By the loss of the book, and the
Bookseller's teasing, he wants only
To travel home. He goes to the market
To find a ride. Ready to go, the
Baaleguleh yells, "Hop in, let's move!"
Amazed, the rabbi wonders, only one fare
And he travels?
"Come up, rabbi, don't worry!"

The baaleguleh high on the driver's seat,
The rabbi under the covered wagon's hood, they travel.
Only an hour or two, he thinks, and I'll
Be home. But soon he feels a halt and
Looking out, he hears the baaleguleh say:
"Come! Crawl out and look at this!"
The rabbi crawls, looks, but cannot even
Recognize the road. "Is this not a strange
Road?" he asks. "It'll get to be your own.
Look!" And he points to a field, peasants
Barefoot, scythes in hand cutting hay;
Fragrant hay! Rolling fields! Vaulted sky!
Bird swarms swooping overhead!
"I see nothing," says the rabbi. "OK! We'll keep trucking!"

Hours pass, suddenly another stop.
"Come on out, rabbi!"
This time, even more alien,
A field and forest. The baaleguleh
Stops to chat with a village peddler.

"Why drag me around?" The rabbi is angry,
But the baaleguleh just says, "This fellow
Can use a ride; move over and we'll
Take him a spell."
The wagon moves on, the peddler and the
Rabbi sitting under the hood.
The rabbi's silence breathes icy anger,
So the peddler keeps his peace and
They move on.

Another stop! Now its a *kuzhnya* (smithy)
In some strange shtetl. The peddler leaves,
Moving on his way. The baaleguleh waits
In the kuzhnya for the *kowal* (blacksmith)
To shoe the horse. He calls outside
To the rabbi: "Come on in, it's happier
Here." At the door of the smithy stands
The rabbi, growling with anger.
"What impertinence! All I need is to overhear
The conversations of kowals and baalegulehs!"

Finally, they travel on. But soon oats are
Needed for the horse, so onto the feedstore.
In friendly conversation stand the storekeeper,
The baaleguleh, and a woman. The rabbi burns
With rage: "When will there be an end to this!"
The baaleguleh looks at him: "It's a good store,
Good folks here, why don't you come in?"
The rabbi bites his lip: even exile will someday
Find its end…

Night falls and they drive up to a *kretchma* (roadhouse).
As the baaleguleh unhitches the horse,
The rabbi starts to go,
Trying to find his colleague in the shtetl.
But he is stopped: "You'll find good people in the roadhouse, too."

The chutzpah of the baaleguleh
Imprisons him and he stays. The kretchma is
Filled with simple folk eating, drinking, smoking.
He finds a corner and prays *Ma'ariv* (the evening prayer).
He lets himself be served supper
While the *kretchmer* and the baaleguleh hum.
Tired of his anger, he naps and knows not
When lamps are doused and where the night got lost.

The day grays to dawn and the baaleguleh shakes him awake.
He wants to wash his hands for prayer.
But the other rushes him: "You'll daven at home."
Now the wagon flies, the road looks familiar.
The sun is fully up, and they are at the rabbi's house.
"Rabbi! We have arrived!"
Feeling fortunate, "Home at last," he reaches for his wallet.
"How much do I owe you?" he asks.
"You owe me nothing," replies the baaleguleh,
"I'll even pay you!" And he pulls out
The book and gives it to the rabbi.
"Take it, rabbi. If you see nothing
And hear nothing, this book won't help you
Either!" He turns to his horse and
Urges him with a "Heigh-Ho!"
The rabbi stands there confused.
He rushes to pursue the wagon,
But the baaleguleh is way gone.

From The Walker (Der Geyer)
By Menachem Boraisha
(Translated from the Yiddish)

NOTE

1 Yiddish for *baal ha'agalah*, literally "master of the wheel," meaning a stagecoach driver.

How the Besht Began

The following is a letter written by the Baal Shem Tov to Reb Mordecai, the hidden saint, a friend and contemporary of the Baal Shem Tov. Since Reb Mordecai was a nistar, a hidden tzadik, we know no more about him. There is serious doubt as to the authenticity of the Besht's letters, yet their content has so deeply informed the Hasidic imagination that historical authenticity is beside the point.

To His Holy Honor, beloved of my soul, silence is praise to him, the pillar of fire, Rabbi Mordecai, the righteous one, may his light radiate:

I have received your letter through our colleague—known to us—and here I am ready to fulfill the wish of your holy honor, the Prince of Torah, the man of God who dwells in the country of Tartary, and I shall disclose to the ears of your holy honor the known causation from the beginning on, how the Name-Blessed-be-He has brought me to now. (As it is known to Your Holy Honor, I meditate in solitude in the field and I do not have large sheets of paper, only these small pieces which are so thin that they blot. Therefore, I am forced to write only on one side of the paper.)

I was born in the holy city of Okkup in the year 5458 [1698]. At the time when I was five years old, I was orphaned of my father and my mother of blessed memory (may others be protected from this) and I remained cast at the expense of the congregation in matters of food, drink, and clothes, and also concerning tuition. But as soon as the heads and leaders of the city noted that there was no sign of blessings in my studies, they forsook me, and I went from city to city and from settlement to settlement, until I came, with the help of the Name-Blessed-be-He, to the holy city of Brody. It was then that I turned eighteen years old and was made a tutor of children, and there was the Holy Master, Rabbi Gershon, may his light radiate, in whose house there grew up an orphan whom he gave to me to tutor in Torah. It was thus that it turned out that I became his brother-in-law, since my wife, may she live, is his sister. I did not know at all that I had a "high" soul, thank God, in the merit of my holy fathers. It was once in Brody, on a Friday of *Vayeshev* [Winter, 1716], at one past noon, I fell into a trance, and there came to me an old man in my dreams who said to me, "Little Israel, do you know who I am?" And I answered, "No." And he said to me: "Know that I was sent to you from heaven to teach you. No one is to know of this, not even your wife. Therefore, every day, you should go between the great mountains and I will come to you and teach you. I will disclose to you everything concerning your demeanor, God willing. Of this dream you shall not tell anyone, God forbid, until I will so command you." I asked him what his name was and he answered me, "In time, God willing, you will become aware of everything." These were the words of that old saint. Immediately he disappeared. I awoke. In my heart, I imagined that it was only a dream I need not take seriously, just like any other dream. Immediately I went to bathe in honor of the Sabbath.

Just as I dipped my head in the mikvah to be completely immersed, I opened my eyes and saw him in the pool (such is my way that in the water I open my eyes) and a tremendous awe and fear befell me. I felt that I was turned into another person. From that time on, a spirit of holiness would engulf me at the time of the reception of the holy Sabbath. I saw that the people of the community looked at me differently. I did not know what made them do this. It was during the night of the holy Sabbath that that venerable one came to me again in a dream (he is my master and my teacher, who is known to his holy honor, may his light radiate). He said to me: "Yisrolikel, do not think that it was a mere dream today. Know for sure that it is completely true. And the sign is that Sunday, God willing, you will go to the outskirts of the city and you will find me between the second and the third hills. However, for Heaven's sake, on Sunday before you come, you must immerse yourself in the mikvah four times." He disappeared, and as I awoke from my sleep, I understood that things were not quite as simple as they seemed, that this was not a mere dream but a heavenly thing. It must all be in the merit of my holy parents of blessed memory. They must have exerted themselves in much prayer and intercession which they put before the throne of Glory that Heaven should have mercy on me that I might merit to come to so high a rung. Thus I understood it. At the morning service of the Holy Sabbath, they called me to the Torah to read the *maftir* [final and prophetic portion of Torah reading]. This was even more marvelous in my eyes, for never had I thus been honored in the congregation. My brother-in-law, the holy master, may his light radiate, used to conduct the calling to the *aliyot* [Torah reading] by himself.

And thus it was that at the time of the third meal of the Holy Sabbath, in the house of my holy brother-in-law, may his light radiate, that he called me to his place and said to me, "Yisrolik, what is it that I notice in you? I see a great change on your face. Are you by any chance, God forbid, not in perfect health?" But I did not answer him at all, just as my teacher and holy master commanded me. At the conclusion of the Sabbath, after havdalah in my house, just as I was singing Elijah's hymn, my wife, may she live, asked me, "Why is it that you are so pale?" Yet I did not answer her either.

Here it was Sunday, *Parshat Miketz,* and a heavy blizzard came down. Yet I did what I had to do and at the hour before noon I went to immerse in the mikvah, and afterwards I immediately went to the outskirts of the city. Since I wore a heavy fur, I felt warm. It was about five miles to the second mountain. Meanwhile, a gentile traveling from the city on a sleigh took pity on me, and invited me to share the ride. As we neared the place of meeting between the second and the third hill, I descended from the sleigh and walked into the vale between the two hills. Suddenly, the venerable one, my teacher and holy master, faced me and said, "Follow me." I went after him and suddenly a door opened to a cave in the cleft of a rock, and behold, it was full of light. Inside there was a table and two chairs. My holy teacher and master sat on the first chair and said to me: "Sit, my child." And I sat in the second chair. He took a book from his pocket, the name of which I must not yet disclose, but of a truth I tell you, it was the first time that I ever saw this holy book. He began from the beginning and said to me, "My son, look." His face was shining and dazzling like stars, and really it was like a supernal soul had entered into me. I began to read the book out loud, and he lifted his hands above my head in blessing. And I, although I had not seen this holy book in all my days, found immense understanding in it. My eyes began to be illumined and the paths of Heaven were shown before me. The gates of understanding were really opened to me, exactly like at the revelation at Mount Sinai. In about two hours he said to me, "My child, enough. God willing, tomorrow you will again come and will then find me in the cave just as you did today. But God forbid that you tell anyone of this." So I asked my teacher and holy master, "What is your name?" He answered me, "It is not yet time that you should know. When the time is right, you will become aware of it by yourself." He took me by the right hand and we both went out of the holy cave together. He accompanied me to the gate of the city. There he put his two holy hands on my head and blessed me, but I was not able to hear the blessing letter by letter. Thus it was also on the morrow, and for about a whole year, and yet I still did not know the name of my holy teacher.

Once during the summer before we took leave of one another, near the gate of the city, he told me his name, and due to the great fear and awe that fell on me, realizing that I merited to receive Torah and learning from so holy and awesome a master, I fell in a faint to the ground until, with the help of the Name-Blessed-be-He, I was brought back to my health. He then said to me that I must change the place of my dwelling from a city to a village, and then, with the help of God, and with the efforts of my brother-in-law, the sainted princely master, may he live, I changed the place of my dwelling to a village near Kittov. There, I established an inn, and I, from Sabbath to Sabbath, was in meditation and solitude until this very day, spending my time between the mountains. Every Sabbath eve, I returned to my house. Every day of the week, I received the privilege of facing my holy teacher and master, and he has disclosed to me the secrets of the mysteries, until, thank God, no secret escapes me. But this causes me pain. It is already a month since one day my holy teacher and master came to me at the time of the morning watch [between two and six a.m.] and said to me: "Yisrolikel, you know, my child, that the time will soon come when you must be revealed. Since thus it was decreed, written, and signed from Heaven that when you become thirty-six years old, you must be revealed."

The Letter of Reb Adam Baal Shem

This letter, subject to the same reservations as the last, is a fragment written by the legendary master Reb Adam Baal Shem, who is said to have a mystical connection with the Baal Shem Tov. A copy of this letter was sent by the Besht to his brother-in-law Reb Gershon of Kittov. It is believed to have been addressed, and thus refers, to the Besht himself.

I have heard from our teacher and master, the holy one, and I quote: In the year 5333 [1572] there lived in the holy city of Safed (may it be rebuilt speedily in our days, amen) a simple, pious Jew who was only able to daven and not more. (Torah study was beyond him.) Yet he was perfect in his deeds and was one who lived humbly, not attracting people's attention.

Once at night, when he was performing the midnightly prayer, he heard a knock at the door. Asking who it was, the other answered that he is Elijah the Prophet, may he be remembered for good, so he admitted him into the house.

Just as he came into the room to be with him, a luminous glow filled even the corners. There was such great joy and elation that even the little children began to dance in their cribs.

Said the Jew to Elijah, "Sit, rabbi, may you live." Elijah sat down and said to the Jew, "I came to you to reveal the year of the advent of the Messiah! But only on the condition that you tell me one thing. Namely, what did you do on the day of your bar mitzvah? For, on account of your deed, it was decreed from above that you should merit to have me reveal myself to you, and to reveal the hidden mysteries."

Thereupon the Jew answered, "Whatever I have done, I have done it only for His Blessed Name's sake. How then can I reveal this to anyone except to His Blessed Name? But, in case his holy honor, my teacher and master, will, on account of my refusal, not reveal these exalted things to me, I do not need them. I have it by tradition that whatever a Jew does, he should hide it from others so that it may be only for the sake of His-Blessed-Name alone."

Suddenly, Elijah disappeared from him. Above, there was a great tumult on account of this man's simplicity, that he refused Elijah the Prophet, in order that his deed be only for the sake of Heaven.

So it was decreed with the agreement of the entire heavenly tribunal that Prophet Elijah must nevertheless reveal himself to him, and teach him Torah and reveal to him the hidden mysteries. And so it was.

Elijah revealed himself to him and taught him many secrets of the Holy Torah. He became the outstanding one in his generation and a perfect tzadik in hiding. No one knew of his holiness and greatness.

And it was that day when, at the time of his old age, he left this world, they set him a place above in the heavenly mansion where the holy fathers are. But the advocates-of-good made a tumult, saying that he deserves an even greater reward, because he was such a great tzadik, and he hid himself that no one should know of his greatness, and all that he did, he did in the truthmost truth for the sake of Heaven alone. Thus he deserves an immensely great reward. In response, the tribunal of Heaven decreed as follows:

> Being that the world did not merit to sense the fragrance of the spirit of his Torah, therefore this holy soul shall once again come to this lowest world and this time Heaven shall force this soul to reveal herself. So a new Way shall be

> revealed through this soul and all the world shall be filled with knowledge in order to bring the End nearer.

And so it was.

Now I shall reveal to you, in the name of our teacher and holy master, that your honored holiness, may you live, is this holy soul and that you have come to this world for a second time in order to scent the world with fragrance and purify it with the spirit of purity and the spirit of holiness. Thus very soon must you reveal yourself and illuminate the heart of everyone with New Light. The name of Heaven will be sanctified through your hand and the redemption brought near speedily in our day. Amen, thus be the Will.

From the Teachings of Reb Pinchas of Koretz (*Midrash Pinchas*)

Rabbi Pinchas Shapira Koretz (1720–1801) was a disciple of the Besht and a disciple-colleague of the Maggid of Mezeritch, Dov Baer. His way was nondualistic (when compared to many of his colleagues) and shamanistic.

Someone asked Reb Pinchas: "How can we pray for someone else to repent when this prayer, if granted, would curtail another person's freedom of choice? Is it not said by the Rabbis that everything is in heaven's hands, except the fear of heaven?" He answered: "What is God? The totality of souls. Whatever exists in the whole can also be found in a part. So, in any one soul, all souls are contained. If I turn, in teshuvah, I contain in me the friend whom I wish to help, and he contains me in him. My teshuvah makes the him-in-me better and the me-in-him better. This way, it becomes so much easier for him-in-him to become better."

•

A man can live in the same house with a tzadik and still be stupid. What can you expect me to say? If you hear one word, you think you know it all already? The brakhah is not found in what is manifest to everyone's eyes. What is brakhah? The very mystery of the Shekhinah, that's what the Zohar calls the true blessing. Do you want to know when you have the brakhah? When all the chambers of the body vibrate with it. There are things on which the fate of half of this planet depends. If I were to talk about it, even one word, it could all become spoiled and never bear fruit.

·

There are clouds that hover over the mind. To disperse the clouds, you need wind. The wind to disperse the clouds of the mind comes from the movements of prayer, the in-and-out from the lungs, this the Zohar calls ru'ach, spirit, breath. Oy, if I had told of this some years ago, people would have served God by breathing and all the clouds would have dispersed. Yet today I talk and no one takes it to heart.

·

The Zohar says that the gall is the door to hell within. The gates to heaven are the eyes and fountains of the heart. A person has it in his power to place a belt between one and the other and be in touch with the heart and not with the gall.

·

When I must reprove a man, I tell him something gentle and wise. This helps him get in touch with his soul. The soul gives life to its owner, and so he begins to live the soul life. This is what Cordovero[1] says in his *Pardes*. Sometimes I help him get in touch with his soul by telling him a joke. Still, there are those in this generation of ours who preach morals at people, urging them to repent. But the poor man they preach to has no way to help himself to get to teshuvah if they don't help him get in touch with his living soul. This is so important. In fact, this is all new.

·

Whatever is precious in this world is also scarce. There are so few who know how to learn. Tzadikim are even more scarce. Scarcer even are those who really know how to pray. The higher worlds just don't want to come down.[2]

·

In the *Tikkunei Zohar*, it is stated: "Hidden worlds that can be revealed and hidden worlds that cannot be revealed." There are deep insights one ought not to reveal at all. For, in talking about them, one causes God to withdraw vitality from those insights. Now, if a person, in talking about them, could say them with all the feelings of love and awe alive in him, God would not withdraw energy from those insights. But this is extremely difficult for those who have not learned to offer their feelings along with their speech. But if a person serves God with this hidden insight for at least half a year, he has thereby moved himself, and the whole world, toward the scale of merit. Then he has accumulated so much power in it, that, even if he talks openly about it, God's blessing will not be withdrawn from it. Try to understand this deeply.

·

All scripture is holy and is the connecting link between this world and the higher worlds. Hence each person can understand according to the world to which they are connected. However, the Song of Songs is not at all understandable by the mind. It is sacrosanct and connects this world to the Eyn Sof, which is beyond all worlds.

NOTES

1 Rabbi Moshe Cordovero preceded Isaac Luria as the teacher of the Safed Kabbalistic school. Among other works, he is the author of *The Palm Tree of Deborah*.

2 It is in their nature to attract the seekers upward to themselves rather than to descend to lower planes.

Gleanings of Reb Nachman's Counsels (*Likkutei Eitzot*)

Rebbe Nachman of Breslov, a great-grandson of the Baal Shem Tov, was a contemporary of Rebbe Pinchas. He established a unique Hasidic school that during his lifetime emphasized direct prayer in one's vernacular language and the nonexistence of despair. After the leader's death, his followers—in contrast to other Hasidic groups—emphasized the continued accessibility of Rebbe Nachman, and other Hasidic groups thus dubbed his followers "dead Hasidim."

The genius of Rebbe Nachman is so manifold and complex that no short generalization can satisfy those who have become acquainted with his works at greater depth.

There is likelihood that during his travels he encountered Sufism. On his trip to the Holy Land, he cloistered himself for many hours with a young Ishmaelite, perhaps a dervish.

Very diligent must one's search be for the true tzadik. A true tzadik is he who possesses the quality of ru'ach hakodesh [the holy spirit]. The root of perfect faith is the belief in the creation of the world and this belief comes to one through the true tzadik. The root of faith lies in the analysis and separation of the power of illusion—and no one but the true tzadik who possesses ru'ach hakodesh can accomplish that. Thus by destroying illusion he strengthens faith in the creation and renewal of the world. Everyone on earth, from the smallest to the greatest, must take care to search for such a true tzadik all of their life.

For the Torah does not address itself to the dead, meaning those who do not really want to find "life," those who do not take heed for their soul, seeking its redemption forever. The Torah addresses itself only to those who want to be saved from the emptiness and purposelessness in this life and the others.

And so, even if he did merit to find a rebbe or a friend who received guidance from a true tzadik who received living words of truth, and who can helpfully speak to the condition of his soul, he nevertheless must continue seeking.

And even if he succeeded in correcting something in himself, he still must continue seeking, since man does not stand still. Since so many actions do not have the effect one had intended them to have, especially in our day and age, as we so well know in our hearts, one must continue to seek for the true tzadik who possesses ru'ach hakodesh. It is not the search for the bodily appearance of the tzadik that is important. One must search for his ru'ach hakodesh. For only his ru'ach hakodesh is able to isolate and destroy the power of illusion. Illusion was created in order to be separated and refined by the ru'ach hakodesh of the true tzadik. One who has not yet found him must surely seek him out on one's hands and feet, with all one's strength, and all over the world, for all of one's days, in the hope that one will be able to find him and through him find the "life of one's soul," if only for one day, or one hour before one's death.

And even if he did "find" the tzadik, he must continue to be a seeker, for his soul is still dark and he does not yet feel delight in the truth of the tzadik's holy counsel, and so is still far from his tikkun [cosmic repair]. For the finding of the ru'ach hakodesh of the tzadik is the important thing. He who would sincerely seek the tzadik would surely find him, for "God does not require the impossible from his creatures, and he who says that he sought and found is to be believed" (Babylonian Talmud, Megillah 6b).

Even the true teacher himself must seek and search in order to rediscover the holiness of his own master's ru'ach hakodesh that he has received, until he will again find himself. Thus he will truly be able to guide, counsel, and speak to the conditions of the people coming to him. For it is extremely difficult to counsel and help anyone possessing "free choice." Only by the amazing graces of God that the tzadik draws down from the upper worlds to this world, and true merit from below, is it made possible to counsel. Thus, in working with people to bring them to themselves, one must work in great depth, a depth scarcely imaginable. Therefore, one must seek and search and plead with one's master, a friend, or a disciple, and only then can one find the ru'ach hakodesh.

·

The Word has immense power. It is even possible to influence a gun with one's words, to make it unable to fire.

·

There is no counsel for anyone who desires to fall asleep except to cease to desire it. The more one desires sleep, the greater will be the resistance. He who pursues sleep will find sleep fleeing. This holds true in anything else. Everything flees us upon our pursuit.

·

The power of reciting the Psalms resides in that man can find himself in each Psalm. All the wars that King David prays about are one's own wars with the evil one and his hosts, and one can find himself in these prayers. Even as David says, "Guard my soul for I am a Hasid," each person must also refer to themselves. For each person is duty bound to judge themselves as being worthy of merit. Each person must find something deserving, a point of goodness within themselves. It is out of this point that they can say of themselves that they truly are a Hasid. Don't we begin our morning prayers with, "What are we, what is life?" and we make ourselves very small and then we say, "But we are Thy people, the children of the covenant." Thus we find Jehoshaphat described (II Chron. 17:6): "He raised his heart in the ways of YHVH." In the ways of the Lord, he raised his heart.

From Reb Nachman's *Meshivat Nefesh* (Soul Retrieval)

If you want to return to the Blessed One, you must become an expert in halacha,[1] so that nothing in the world can overcome you as you rise or fall.

No matter what may befall you, you must remain steadfast and faithful, fulfilling the principle, "If I rise to Heaven, there art Thou; if I spread myself on the bottom of the abyss, there art Thou!" For God is even in the bottomless pit; you can always approach Him.

Also, you must be proficient in "the forward surge" and "the backward draw." In these two ways you have to be an expert in halacha. Wishing to yield yourself again to His Blessed Name, gird your loins and hold tenaciously to the ways of God forever.

Whether you have been granted a higher or a lower rung, you must not be content to remain there, but always aspire upward. Believe and know! It is necessary and possible for you to go on and on. In this process, if you should fall to a lower rung—even into the "bottomless pit"—you must not despair. No matter what happens to you, wherever you may be, and to the very best of your ability, seek His Blessed Name. For it is here that one can also cleave unto Him. And in this consists the expertness of "drawing backward."

Thus to merit repentance and returning, become expert in these two ways of halacha: "surging forward," desiring and working always to be on a yet higher rung toward God; and "drawing backward," holding fast to His Blessed Name, no matter if you fall or what station in life may be granted you. When you have become skilled in this, you will realize that His Right Hand is always extended to receive penitents, who in contrition for their sins have amended their lives.

·

The essence of His greatness is revealed when those who have strayed very far from Him return again to serve Him. In this, the preciousness of His Name is made manifest on Earth as it is in Heaven. Therefore, let no man, due to his estrangement, despair of coming to serve Him. No matter how far you have parted from Him, even the worst sins and evils cannot separate you from Him. On the contrary, it is you who must witness Him in this condition and behold His greatness.

·

Those who congregate with a true tzadik, in fellowship, entering with him in covenant and holding fast to him, must continually arouse in one another [a desire to seek out and serve God]. However, their greatest reassurance flows from the immense power which the true tzadik possesses. His power is so great that he can raise the most damaged soul. Even the soul which has not yet been released from the realm of the unholy forces, and not moved even by a hair's breadth, can be lifted and renewed for good by his great power. In this lies the root of all reassurance. The most amazing graces and blissful hopes are open to him who holds fast to the true tzadik. In the fellowship of friends, with their mutual arousal to serve God, each reminds the other of the counsels, directions, and guidance received from the tzadik, which, by application, they learn to value and understand.

·

Know that His Blessed Name takes great pride in the most frivolous seeker and even in the rebellious sinner. For the Holy One rejoices over him in particular, as He rejoices over all His people. It is therefore forbidden to despair oneself of Him, for God's love and fondness are never separated from us. Consequently, even the greatest sinner can always return. Men of truth are able to find, uncover, and make manifest the inner good and reality in each person, and can bring each man back to His Holy Name.

·

This has to be well understood! Before a man can be raised from rung to rung, he must first fall. For then he can strengthen himself in the service of the Lord, and not become downcast as a result of all the falls and degradations in the world. If one grows stronger and pays no heed to his falls, regardless of what happens to him, he will realize that the purpose of all these falls is the ascent. Therefore, every descent carries an ascent within itself. Anyone who has fallen from his place may think our words do not speak of him but, instead, only of those who are on higher rungs and always proceed upward from rung to rung. He believes that these persons will certainly not fall to so low a level as his own. But he is wrong. Believe and know that everything is said even to the very smallest and lowest person, for God is always compassionate.

·

If a person occupying even the very lowest rung—even if he were standing in the very center of the earth—begins to serve the Lord and enters into the gates of holiness, he will immediately find all sorts of opposition and resistance within himself. For the klippot will send their entire arsenal of passions, illusions, thoughts, and confusions to create intervening obstacles to prevent him from rising. There are many good Hasidim to whom this occurs, and then they think they have fallen. But it is not a fall at all. It is simply that the great arsenal of evil has come to obstruct his path. The opposition, which reared itself, is necessary for his further ascent. It threatens the penitent with more strength than he has to oppose it and blocks his way. Therefore, one has to brace oneself greatly in order not to be downcast or discouraged by this at all. These obstacles are presented so that one may break them and thus be enabled to enter into the higher good.

·

If you still find it difficult to break through whatever great obstruction opposes you, then give *tzedakah* [charity]. Whoever gives tzedakah to the poor causes God to take pride in His children. And through His pride, a person is able to find the strength to destroy the obstacles that oppose him at each rung.

·

One ought always to be happy that he merited to be of the seed of Israel [the God-wrestlers]. And he has great cause to rejoice in having come close to such people of truth, who lead and teach the way of truth. Being fully aware that, ultimately, all will be good, one can enter into the battle with joy and break down all the obstacles that present themselves at each level.

·

In overwhelming the obstacles facing him, and rising from rung to rung, man is also doing a great favor to his fellow. Since it is impossible for two persons to occupy the same level, he must move from rung to rung, so that the man whose rung is just below his can move upward. And so, one's own effort also becomes a boost for one's friend.

·

Do not be downcast when evil thoughts threaten you, for it is through blocking these thoughts that you can mend yourself and effect your teshuvah. Because you now reject such thoughts, you show that your turning was permanent. By rejecting them, you can free the sparks which, through the damage of the covenant, had fallen into such darkness.

·

The whole world is filled with God's glory! Know this. You can find God's Divinity in everything, as He gives existence to all things. And since God is there, invested in all sorts of paradoxical garments and mazes, He rejoices when you find Him because you set Him free.

·

Drowned in evil and the klippot, and on the very lowest level, you will believe it impossible to approach God, simply because you have become so removed from Him. Know, however, that even now you can find His Divinity, and at that very place where you are, He is, and you can become united with Him. Right there you are able to turn to Him with a perfect teshuvah, for, though He wears many more garments there, He is never far from you.

·

A person who has transgressed many times has fallen to the category of "the midst of the eclipse." So he feels there is no more hope. Trespass has been added to sin until these offenses now seem to him to be perfectly permissible. This is called the "first eclipse." When he has further transgressed, then God becomes eclipsed and hidden from him. This is more severe and it becomes truly difficult to find Him. But through the study of Torah, he may be roused to realize God is still with him, so that he can return to truth and approach His Blessed Name. This power and truth are given to the true tzadikim. They can bring anyone, anywhere, near to God.

·

In the lowest places, which seem so remote from His Blessed Name, there especially the supremely High Life is invested. This is the mystery of the Torah. He who has fallen so low knows he can come close to His Blessed Name even in this infernal place. If he will only merit to return from this remote place, then His Blessed Name becomes manifest through him, and many mysteries and secrets of the Torah are revealed.

·

When a person is roused to teshuvah, and he wants to begin to serve the Lord and to travel to a tzadik, simultaneously a greater *yetzer hara* [evil impulse] is aroused. In order to overwhelm this new inclination for evil, one must draw greatly on his strength. So when the person becomes roused to travel and to seek counsel of the true tzadikim, his yearning and longing are very great. But the moment he begins his preparations for traveling, this longing disappears. This is because in making travel preparations, he also creates a new yetzer hara. Therefore, in order to approach His Blessed Name, one must release new energies in himself to overwhelm the yetzer hara anew, for it is a completely new yetzer hara, one that has never yet been confronted.

·

There are all kinds of evil impulses. Most people have a yetzer hara which is very low and vulgar and brutal. Anyone with some subtle knowledge, who is somewhat aware of the greatness of his Creator, will realize this first kind of yetzer hara is a great folly. Any kind of vulgar passion must seem like so much folly in the eyes of a person with some bit of spiritual subtlety. Consequently, this person has to fend against a much higher kind of yetzer hara, as subtle as he.

There is a yetzer hara of the subtlest form, an almost diaphanous shell. This type of yetzer hara is incited against people who have already achieved some level of higher attainment. But even in that subtlety, this yetzer hara is not like the yetzer hara of the tzadikim, for their yetzer hara is a holy angel.

There is a yetzer hara that drives a person close to His Blessed Name, sometimes with great fire and passion. This drive, greater than it ought to be, is of the yetzer hara and of the category "Lest they will force themselves to ascend to the Lord." One has to supplicate and arouse great miracles in order to be also saved from this yetzer hara!

NOTE

1 Literally "walking"; colloquially, "Jewish Law."

From Reb Nachman's *Sichot* (Informal Talks)

This world has no being for man except in that it brings him toward his eternal purpose. Regardless of whether one does or does not have any money, one will spend one's life in equal conditions because the world tends to deceive us entirely. The world deludes man to think that he can really gain profit. In the end, nothing remains of his toil. This can be seen in reality. The majority of men busy themselves working days and years, buying and selling, and yet in the balance they remain with nothing on hand. Even if one does make money, he is eventually removed from it.

The two, man and money, cannot coexist, for either the money is taken from man or man is taken from the money. No one remains together with his money forever. Where is all the money that was made during all the years of the world's existence? People have always made money, yet where is it? The fact is that money has no existence...

·

In serving God, I know of no one who can say that he deserves His Blessed Name according to His greatness. Anyone who merited to realize even the smallest glimpse of God's real greatness will be unable to say that he truly *serves* God. There is neither angel nor seraph who could pride itself that it serves the Lord. The only important thing is that there be the will to serve. One's will ought to be strong and tenacious to come close to Him, be He praised. Although everyone wills and desires this, not all wills are equal, for there are many kinds of will. Depending on the moment, the will of the same person has changed and it seems as if he were another person. This shows that even in the same person, there are many kinds of will. The rule is that there must be a willingness and a longing—to long always—for Him. It is out of one's willingness and longing that one prays, studies, and obeys the commandments. (For in reality, according to His Greatness all these actions are nothing at all, but merely "as if" gestures.)

·

All the "wisdoms," "-ologies," and "-osophies" are nothing at all. The only real being is "simplicity" and "uncomplicatedness." But even in simplicity one must not be a fool. Still, there is no need for clever tricks.

Also, it is not good to be "old"—not even an "old Hasid" or an "old tzadik." "Old"-ness is not good at all, for every day one must be "renewed." One must begin anew at all times. Yes, there is something that does become better the older it gets, but that is something else that, as our sages said, increases in strength.

·

Since the "world" is nothing, what must one do? In order to know this, one needs Heaven's mercies. But for true seekers, they are already blessed since they, through the Torah, already know *what* to do.

·

The "world" preaches that one ought not be overambitious. But I tell you that one must be just that—overambitious. Each must have as his greatest ambition to search and look for the very greatest tzadik and very greatest rebbe and have him be his own Master.

·

Now, about the passions that disturb man. In reality, there is no such thing as a "passion." For food and drink are bodily needs and it is necessary to beget children. All this man is forced to do. There really is no "passion" as long as these are done in purity and holiness. Man's mind is capable of withstanding all "passions." "God gives wisdom to the wise." Everyone has the potential of wisdom. What is necessary is to bring the "potential" into the "actual." This wisdom is by creation given to every man. God grants even more wisdom to those who use it. With it, man can withstand all "passions." Even those who have already been drawn into "passions," and transgressed whatever they transgressed, whose minds have become tainted, confused, and diminished to a point—even they can withstand temptation. The one small point of mind remaining can withstand the whole world and its passions. For at any place, one can be near to God, be He praised. Even in Gehinom, one can come close to God and serve Him in truth.

·

There is one thing that requires great mercy from Him or immense effort, or even both, and that is to reach the point where the fermenting sediment clouding one's consciousness settles down and the mind is at rest and at a standstill, so that one ceases to desire anything in the world in order that everything may be equally unaffecting.

·

"When thou walkest, she will lead you. When thou liest down, she will guard you. When thou wakest, she will make thee talk." This means that everything is the same. For *She,* the Torah, *will lead you* as you walk through this world *and when thou liest* in the grave, there, too, she *shall guard* you, for God and His Torah are also there—*and when thou wakest up* in the World to Come, there too. Since he has no passions except for God and His Torah, all is equal to him. Everywhere he is, he cleaves to God; in this world, in the grave, and in the other World. He who is bound to this world *does* find differences, for this world is wide and the grave is narrow. But to him whose mind is clear of the cloud of the fermenting sediment, all is equal.

·

The glory of God radiates from all beings. The whole world is full of His glory. Even from the tales of the gentiles, His glory comes forth. For His glory always sounds out and beckons man to come close to God. And He, be He praised, will with great mercy and great love and endearment bring the seeker close to Himself. This at times causes man to be so aroused in his prayers that he begins to pray with *hitlahavut* (ecstasy) and great desire to the point where his prayer flows from his lips and his mouth in all willingness. This is the *Light* in which God wraps Himself, for He Himself is the beginning and the prayer. And so it is that man can pray.

·

Even if at times His Blessed Name removes His Presence from man, man must pray and catapult his prayers after Him. This is the category of "Cast thy bundle upon the Lord." For when God removes Himself, one must throw oneself after Him in prayer. As the Zohar states, "He who knows how to shoot arrows," which means the prayers directed after Him.

·

In meditation on Torah or a scriptural verse, one must repeat the thought many, many times, knocking and pounding on the door, until it will be opened. Sometimes a holy thought fleetingly passes through the mind and then one needs great persistence to pursue it.

·

Know that there are great powers in man. By thought alone one can achieve a great deal. Even monetary inflation is the result of the power of mere thought.

·

Thought, by fixing itself upon a thing, causes it to become so. In other words, if the external and internal thought, as well as the very point of awareness, are fastened onto a thing and have taken hold of it—and they did so without disturbance and turning to another thought—this concentration makes things turn out just as first thought to be. This concentration must be down to the most minute detail and not merely in a general way. He must concentrate so that, if the thing became so, it would, for example, in this detail become thus and in that particle so. But he who merely scans, in a general way, is like one who fashions only the outer form of a vessel without creating any open space on the inside.

·

Even in study, a powerful thought is of help, as long as the thought is strong and truly takes hold of its content. For example, a scholar will form the image in his mind of meriting to study and learn the Scriptures or all the Codes together with their major commentaries. He will think and describe to himself fully *how* he will study and how much time (five pages a day, for instance), in order to finish his cycle of learning in one year's time. In this way, he will force his mind with great power and tenacity to go into it fully. He will long and yearn and think about this a great deal and with great force. Then he will surely merit that it will, in reality, become just so. And this is what the sages meant by: "Thought is effective."

·

He who does not obey and listen to the true *chakhmim* [wise ones, sages] can lose his mind, for the root of the madness of the insane is that he does not obey and listen to the sensible ones. For the insane, if he were to obey and listen to the sensible, would not be insane at all. To his disturbed mind, it seems clear that he must tear his garment and wallow in the dirt. If only he were to surrender his mind and will to one who is greater than himself, his madness would be surrendered and annihilated. Thus it is clearly established that the root of insanity is one's inability *to hear* and *obey* the words of the wise. This must be well understood.

Dreams of Reb Nachman

There are some exceptional dreams in Hasidic literature, dealing primarily with the process of the Rebbe's self-knowledge. Reb Nachman of Breslov recorded his own dreams or told them to his disciple Reb Nathan, who recorded them.

In the winter of his thirty-eighth year, the Breslover said: In my dream I sit in my house and no one enters. The thing so amazed me, I went into the other two rooms and there was no one there. So I went outside and I saw that people were standing in circles and whispering about me. This one is mocking me and this one winks knowingly in my direction and this one laughs and this one shows chutzpah against me, and so forth. Even among those who were my Hasidim, there were some who were against me. Some of them looked at me with scorn and whispered against me.

I called one of my men and asked him, "What is this?" He answered me: "How could you have done such a thing, how could you have done such an awful sin?" I did not know at all what they were talking about, and why they were making fun of me, so I looked for that man that he should go and gather a group of my people. When he came back, I considered what to do. I decided to travel to a different country. I came there and even there, there were people standing in circles and whispering about me. Even they had gotten to know the thing. So I went and sat down in some forest. Five of my Hasidim came with me. They sat with me, we sat there, and as we needed something to eat, we sent one of the men to buy it. So

I asked him, did they already stop making all that noise against me? He said that the tumult was as great as it was before.

An old man came and said to me that he wanted to speak to me. I went with him and he said, "How could you do such a thing? Are you not ashamed before your ancestors, your grandfather, Reb Nachman, your great-grandfather, the Baal Shem Tov? Why aren't you ashamed before the Torah of Moses and the holy forefathers, Abraham, Isaac, and Jacob? What do you think, you will continue to stay here? You can't stay here always and, finally, you will not have any more money and you are a weak man. What will you do? Do you think that you can go to another country? Consider—either they know who you are, or they will have heard of your deed. If they don't know who you are, you will not be able to earn your keep." So I said, "Well, if it is so, then what am I to do? Will I have a part in the World to Come?" He said, "Do you think that they will still give you a part in the World to Come? Even Hell is not sufficient for you to hide there, for you have caused a great desecration of the Name." I said to him: "Go away, here I thought that you would console me and speak to my heart, and you bring me such pain, go away."

The old man went away. I feared that since I have been here for a long time, I might forget what I have learned, so I looked for the man whom I sent to buy the victuals, that he would try and get a book for me. He went and could not bring me a book. It was impossible for him to get any book without telling that it was I who needed the book. So I had great pains that I am not only in exile, but that I do not have a book and that I am bound to forget all my studies.

The old man came back and brought a book, and I asked him, "What have you got in your hand?" and he said, "A book," and I said to him, "Could you please lend me the book?" He gave it to me and I took it, and I did not understand even how to hold the book. I opened it and I couldn't even understand the meaning of the words, for it was to me like a strange language in a foreign script. The thing caused me great pains. I was afraid for my own people: if they were to recognize that I cannot even read a book, they, too, will leave me. So the old man called me to come so that he could speak to me.

Again he began to upbraid me for having committed such a grave sin without being ashamed and that even in Hell, there would be no place for me to hide. I said to him, "If one of the souls from the higher world would have told me such a thing, I would believe him." He said to me: "I am from there," and he proved to me that he was from there, and I remembered the story of the Baal Shem Tov who, too, had thought at one point that he had lost his part in the World to Come, and he had said:

"I love Him, whose Name be blessed, even without reward in the World to Come!"

And I cast my head backward with great bitterness, and as I cast my head backward, there gathered about me all the great people, and the old man said to me that I should be ashamed before them, before my grandfather and all the forefathers. And they said to me the sentence: "The fruit of the earth is for beauty and for pride." They said to me: "We are very proud of you." And they brought to me all my people and children. All of them consoled me greatly. With such great bitterness had I cast my head back that even he who had transgressed the entire Torah would have been forgiven for it. And the rest of the good I don't tell you, though it truly was good.

·

The thirty-seventh year, [the night of] the first candle of Hanukkah, after the lighting of the Hanukkah candle, I dreamt that a stranger came and asked me, "How do you make your living?" and I said, "My livelihood is not located in my home, it comes to me from outside." He asked me, "What do you study?" and I told him, and we began to speak of Torah. We began to speak like friends with things that issue from the heart and I began to yearn and to muse, "How does one reach any rung in holiness?" and my guest said, "I will teach you." I began to think, perhaps he is not a human being. So, I sat and thought how he spoke to me like a human being, but then immediately my faith in him became strengthened, and I called him, "Master, rebbe," and I said to him, "Before I begin anything else, I want to know how to honor you properly, so that I will not come to injure the proper honor due to you, for a plain human being would not know what to do. Therefore, I want you to teach me how to honor you properly." He said to me, "I have no time now, I will come another time and teach you this." So I said to him, "Even this I must learn from you. How far must I accompany you?" And he said to me, "Up to the door."

I thought in my mind, "I do not know him, and I do not know who he is," so I said to him, "I am afraid to go with you." He said to me, "Why are you afraid? Do I not sit and teach you? If I wanted to harm you, who would have stopped me?" And so, I began to walk him to the door. He took hold of me and caused me to fly high and I felt cold. He gave me a garment and said to me, "Take this garment and you will feel good. You will have food and drink and all will be good and you will sit in your home." Suddenly, I saw that I was at home. I did not believe myself, and I looked around and I saw that I was speaking to people. I was eating and drinking like any other human being and then, suddenly, I saw myself flying in the air as before. I sat and saw again that I was at home, and so, back and forth between home and flying above in the air. Then he brought me down into a valley between two mountains. There I found a book. In that book there were all kinds of connections of letters, illustrations of vessels. And the vessels themselves were letters. Inside the vessels were more letters. With these letters that were inside the vessels, one could make such vessels. I wanted to study this book. I began to see that I was again at home, so I returned and found myself once more in the valley. I decided to go up on the mountain path, so that I could find some settled place.

As I ascended the mountain, I saw a golden tree with branches of gold. From the branches hung all sorts of vessels that were like those depicted in the book. Inside of these vessels were other vessels that were made out of these vessels and the letters in them. So I wanted to take the vessels from there but I couldn't, because the thicket did not permit me to get through.

Then I saw myself again in the house and it was very amazing to me that I was sometimes here and sometimes there. I wanted to tell of this amazing thing to the people, but how can you tell them such a thing that is impossible to believe? I looked through the window, and I saw my guest. I asked him to enter, and he said to me, "I have no time for I am going to you." I said to him, "Even this is an amazing thing, for I am here. What does it mean that you are on your way to me?" He said, "The hour when you decided to come with me and accompany me to the door, I took your soul from you and gave her a garment from the lower garden of Eden. All that remained with you was your nefesh [lower soul], and ru'ach [breath-spirit], while I had taken up your neshamah [higher soul]. Therefore, when you raise your thought up to there, that is why you are there, and you receive your illumination from there. When you return here, then you are here." And all this I saw, but I did not know from which world he was; I decided that he truly was from the good world.

And the story has not yet been completed, nor has it found its end.

·

Once, I saw in my dream that I woke up in a forest that was endless and I wanted to return home. One came to me and said, "In this forest one can never come to its end for it is so long that it is infinite and all the instruments and the vessels of this world are made from this forest." He showed me a way to get out of the forest. This way brought me to a river. I wanted to come to the end of the river. A man came and said, "It is impossible to cross the river, for the river is boundless. All the people of this world drink from the source of this river"; but then he showed me a way to go out through the river. Then I came into a mill which stood at the side of the river, and someone came and said to me, "Here is ground the grain for all the people of the world." And I again entered into the forest where I saw a smith working, and entered into the smithy and they told me, "This smith makes the vessels for the whole world."

·

It was Yom Kippur and I dreamed. It was very clear to me at that time that in Heaven every Yom Kippur they [the heavenly hosts] demanded one person's life as a sacrifice. I volunteered. They said to me that I must put it in writing. So I wrote and signed. Then they wanted to offer me up as a sacrifice. I had regrets and wanted to hide. But I saw that a large group of people had gathered around to witness the sacrifice, and I could not hide. So I sought to go out of the city. But as I left the city, I noticed that I had just returned.

So I entered into the city and I tried to hide among the non-Jews. I was afraid that if they were to come and search for me, they would surrender me to be sacrificed. But then there was another tzadik who agreed to be a sacrifice in my place. Nevertheless, I am still afraid of the future.

Guide to Spiritual Progress by Rabbi Moshe Leib of Sassov

Rabbi Moshe Leib of Sassov was a disciple of Reb Shmelke of Nikolsburg, disciple of the Maggid of Mezeritch. Ecstatic in prayer, deeply compassionate in his interpersonal life, he was the hero celebrated by Peretz in his story "If Not Higher." His writing style is noble and in the tradition of medieval scholastic poets. This guide belongs with the literature of spiritual recipes.

If you will cancel out your existence in favor of His Holy Name at the time of prayer, you can be assured that you will not forget Him all day.

Fools they are, who due to their sins castigate their bodies in fasting and cold baths. Keeping yourself from being overwhelmed by anger will do you more good than a thousand fast days.

To hear others insult you and not answer back is better for you than a thousand austerities and castigations.

There are many people who served His Blessed Name all their days and toward the end, they slid back from His service. All their service was for naught. However, seven times the righteous fall and yet still they rise.

At times of such a fall, recall the early days in which you were graciously illuminated. You *did* see eye to eye in real sight the greatness of the Creator and His Exaltedness, and you might ask yourself why you have now changed.

Of course the reason is that you have become involved in purely physical pursuits and that you have not freed yourself.

If the feelings of Love and Awe have become obliterated in you, you can arouse them through things of this world. The desire will catch on and then you will bring it into the service of the Holy.

Holy men I know said to me (concerning this method): "I bethought my way in things of *this* world and brought my feet back to Your Commandments through this."

The "fall" in the tzadik does not result from being engrossed in matter, God forbid, but rather from the lack of joy. It is due to this lack of joy that the feelings of Love and Awe are taken from him.

If only you will begin to enter His Holy Service, you will find that the gates of light will open themselves like the gates of Heaven.

I have heard from a holy person (who interpreted "taste and see that God is good"), "It takes just a small taste, like a man who tastes his food, and then you will see how much good is before you."

Realize at moments of depression that you come from a very high place and that you are hewn from a holy rock.

If your soul becomes committed to the idea that this world was not created for any other purpose, but that through it your soul will reach eternal peace and rest, the abyss will not be able to overpower you.

If your soul has been committed to the fact that you are a servant of a great and holy King whose real praise is silence, how much can you rejoice in this!

This world is something very honored and great, if you learn to use it well. In it, man can reach the life of the World to Come and cause the indwelling of soul within himself; for this world is called "the world of action."

Remove anger from your heart, for anger causes you to dwell in folly.

Realize well that you are a stranger on Earth and, therefore, hold both the good and the not-good as equals.

A sigh breaks one's body.

Why worry over a world that is not yours?

Remember well the saying of the holy person, "What are we?"

There is no gain in permitting your tongue to be your master, for there is no better vessel to contain wisdom than silence.

It is good to be separate—*with* other people.

A holy man once said, "Be a holy people in all your deeds facing God, thus you can raise all earthly things to God."

There is no greater fool than he who spends his life in regrets.

Realize that you do have a place that is yours to occupy, and it is given to you, and no man can take away that which is prepared for his neighbor.

Freedom from bodily constipation brings about freedom of spiritual constipation.

There is really nothing new under the sun. There were already people who studied the Torah day and night and nevertheless, they did not taste the fear of Heaven.

To love your neighbor as your own self is a great principle of Torah.

If you do not fully and truly love your fellow man, you have not yet tasted the true taste of the Awe of His Holy Name.

If you truly believe and have decided in your soul that both the good and evil comes from His Blessed Name, and that nothing else can be done without Him, then it is impossible that you should have pain and anxiety due to the fact that things are done against you [as this is also God's will].

Establish that the Service of God is the most important thing in your life and that the life of this world is only an auxiliary to it. When this will have become decided in your mind, you will see with your eyes the greatness of His Holy Name.

A dull and closed heart cannot see the greatness of His Holy Name, nor His Exaltedness.

Reflect in your mind on all the miracles and wonders that were experienced from the beginning of creation until this very day, and your eyes will become illuminated.

And a holy man once said, "When I was healed from my sickness through medicine taken from roots and herbs, I recognized that the world and all that fills it belongs to God, and that all that He had created, He did for man."

All intelligent souls will realize the impossibility of such a world coming into being without purpose; and thus they will come to recognize that this purpose is man, and that man himself was created with amazing wisdom. This wisdom is so great that all the scientists of nature cannot yet understand it—that all this was made so that man can live fully on earth.

His Holy Name does provide fulfillment of the will of those that fear Him, even without prayer, as soon as He sees what is on their minds.

Consider that it is quite possible that there are such people whose minds you cannot understand, whose knowledge is much broader and deeper and whose actions amaze you, whose reasons you cannot understand.

If the desire for worldly things burns in you, remember who planted this desire in you, that it is His Blessed Name. Thus you will fear and separate yourself from the desire out of awe.

It is important to *know* the God of your father, both in His apparent functions in creation and through the true Kabbalah.

From the Teachings of Reb Mordecai Yosef Leiner of Izbitza

Reb Mordecai Yosef Leiner of Izbitza was a disciple of Reb Yaakov Yitzchak of Peshiska (the Yehudi), Reb Simcha Bunim of Peshiska, and the Kotzker Rebbe. When he and the latter diverged, Reb Mordecai founded his own school. His grandson, Reb Gershon Henoch, reestablished the use of takhelet, *the turquoise-blue dye used for tzitzit, for the first time in 1,400 years. Reb Mordecai's school of Hasidic thought is profoundly unitive, as the reader will see below.*

Anokhi Hashem Elohekha: "I am the Lord your God." It was not said *ani* (I am), though both words [anokhi and ani] mean "I am," for had it been written *ani*, we would have assumed then that the Holy One, blessed be He, revealed to Israel all of His light and perfection, and afterwards they would not have been able to find anything more profound because everything was already revealed. However, since He used the word *anokhi* which includes the letter *kaf*, which grammatically refers to the comparative—that is to say, something *like* that which I am—meaning it does not contain all perfection, but only a likeness that stirs the imagination, which only points to the light that the Holy One, blessed be He, will reveal in the future.

The more a person attains in the profound understanding of the words of Torah, the more he sees that up to now he was in darkness, and this alludes to the flux of night and day. For day is when His Blessed Name opens the Gates of Wisdom to man, and the night points to the fact that no one has ever attained complete perfection. For all that he attains is only like night in comparison to the day that is yet to come; so it goes on forever. Consequently, all is like that night that precedes day, which the Holy One, blessed be He, will open in the future.

For this reason, the commandment "Thou shalt not make thee a hewn god" is attached to the First Commandment, "I am the Lord your God." And as the Zohar puts it, although Moses was commanded to hew for himself the tablets, it nevertheless was said, "Make thee no hewn things," which means, "Make thee no other Torah." The content of the word *hewn* is something that is specific and finite and limited, according to measure and quantity that contains in it all that can be contained. And while this fountain, the Torah, was given to us through Moses, our teacher, peace be upon him, it is not given to the human mind to attain, for such perfection is not part of the mind, which is limited.

And this is what the Gemarah further tells us: that Caesar said to Rabbi Yeshua ben Hananya, "I, too, can make a Torah of Moses," and then he decreed that no fire was to burn in all of Rome for a period of three days. Soon he saw smoke rise from one house. Caesar then said: "One of my officers is ill and he needs to be exempted from the decree." The truth is that even with our Law it is so: as it is taught, for the saving of a life, set the Sabbath aside. However, this is not because the two of them, Sabbath and life, are diametrically opposed, but rather because the Torah itself, by its own Law, demands the precedence of life and the saving of it over the keeping of the Sabbath. Therefore, they are not contradictory, for even to save a life and to set the Sabbath aside is part of the Law of the Torah. And so it is in all occasions when there is something to be done for the Lord, we are told to set the Law of the Torah aside. And though the Torah points to all the exigencies and vicissitudes that are yet to come, it nevertheless has a transcendental light surrounding each Law and every being that can exist that no man can fully attain. And this is the meaning of the Zohar's explanation. "Make thee no hewn image" is an absolute in a positive commandment; "and no picture" is an absolute in a negative commandment, for to man nothing was revealed in its entirety.

"Remember the Sabbath day to keep it Holy, for the Sabbath day is the Sabbath of One Lord." There are two Sabbaths, for all the 613 commandments are called Sabbaths, as the Zohar says. Sabbath is the name of the Holy One, Blessed be He, and when a person is stirred to this desire, to do the will of His Blessed Name, to follow His positive commandments, and to observe the negative commandments, and when he sets this to his heart, it is said that he remembers the Sabbath day. However, there is an overwhelming forgetfulness in which he forgets the Sabbath and the Lord. The knowledge of the Will of His Blessed Name is obscured from him, and he does what he does concerning this. Of this it is said: "Six days he does his work." That is, he removes himself from the Sabbath and forgets. And then the Sabbath comes again, and causes him to return and sets his heart to know what he has done. And then comes the great outcry of his heart, reproving and saying, "What did I do?" For no person comes fully to understand the words of Torah until he first stumbles in them and then he is offered the counsel of sacrifices that bring about atonement. This is the meaning of "Honor thy father and mother." For a person would much sooner blame a parent than his own inner nature. So to this purpose God commands, honor your father and mother: do not blame others to absolve you of your sacrifices, but rather accept your fault and bring the sacrifices that bring about atonement.

•

"Make no God of silver or God of gold for yourself, but an altar of earth build Me, for everywhere where My name is mentioned, there I will come and bless thee." A "God of silver" points to the color of love and to the reflection of burning fervor that is transcendent and is beyond your real being, for His Blessed Name brings about love for man only if it is true and authentic to himself. And a "God of gold" is the color of awe, which is beyond your attainment. But rather, "build an altar of earth" with simplicity as you feel things in your heart; and then "everywhere where My name is mentioned," that is to say, clarify that the point of sincerity is in your heart;

"that you do things for the sake of heaven," there I will send you an influx of increased blessing.

·

"Do not ascend on steps to My altar; do not uncover thy shame." That is to say, do not take pride over any soul in Israel so that their shame be not revealed, for pride over the level of another will cause you to descend to his level, and him to rise. "Make thee no molten god," that is to say, set yourself no mold, no general rule or role, for at a time when you have the understanding of your heart, and it is all clear, then you need not look at general principles, to be guided by them, but you love from the understanding of your heart. You will know how to do every detail as it is in itself, not as it is a part of a general, abstract system.

·

"Do not turn to false gods." This points to a foolish scrupulosity, for the word *elil* [idol] is related to the words *al yad* [near at hand], the tail of which is far removed from the head, and in it, all knowledge is greatly reduced. And this was said to the perfectly righteous, whose heart is drawn after the will of God, to teach them that when a desire for something should come into the heart they need not confine themselves behind so many fences of awe and fear; rather they should allow themselves to do what comes to them, and trust in the Lord that no evil will befall them, as it is written: "Seek not to be overly righteous, nor to be overly wise."

·

"Tell the priests, the sons of Aaron, not to defile themselves by touching the dead." A priest is one who serves the Lord and who sees that everything that happens in the world is not the result of accident, but providence and intention from Him, be He Blessed, and knows that His desire is only to be beneficent to His creatures. But if one was to see things only as accidents, and forget about God's plan in the world, and see just a corpse, then he might lose his way. The Midrash says: "Don't you look at corpses, for that would reduce your joy, and then you would contaminate My joy," for it is the work of the majordomo to bring joy to the king. So, too, it is our task to bring joy to the King of Kings.

·

If all the accidental properties [of a given desire, event, or idea] have been removed, and there is still something that finds favor, it is a sign that there is some good in it. And to this purpose the Torah speaks about the yetzer hara, the evil inclination, for it can happen that the yetzer of a person should so greatly overwhelm him that his choice is completely taken from him and he cannot move, and then it is clear that it comes from God. This we find with Judah and Tamar.

The Torah teaches us this so that no one who has lived through such an experience should feel rejected, but realize that he was an instrument of purpose. This is the blessing that Moses, the man of God, blessed the children of Israel with before his death [expanded awareness of a grander *purpose*]. For His Blessed Name had given everything into the hands of Moses at that time, so that he could bless and order things to the ends of all generations as to what historical happenings would befall Israel. And, depending on this ordering, each soul has to do its service for God and this has to be done before their death. For Moses is the choice of all souls, and on the day of his death all perfection came to him. Similarly, each one attains his perfection in his fullness.

Jacob, our forefather, attained his perfection when he went to Egypt, and those seventeen years that he lived in Egypt were a reflection of the World to Come. So, too, Moses was completed on the day of his death, and then he could bless them, and, because he found his own perfection his blessing made this perfection possible for all Israel.

·

We eat eggs on the night of Pesach because eggs are a sign of mourning, and on Pesach, the infinite light did not come in its fullness; it was only a momentary flash that then again was hidden. Only on Shavuot, when the Torah is given, is the full light revealed. All of this is alluded to by the egg, for the day when the egg is laid, the chick is not yet born. It needs a warm brooding-over before it can attain life of its own.

Chaim VaChesed (Life and Grace) by Reb Chaim Haikel of Amdur

Reb Chaim Haikel of Amdur, a disciple of the Maggid, was an ecstatic who taught among "Litvaks" (literally, "Lithuanians"), that is, people who considered themselves intellectuals in Torah. He managed to move them to great fervor. His way shares much with that of Reb Pinchas of Koretz.

When taking leave, people drink a toast to each other and say "l'chaim." Rebbe Chaim Haikel's teachings will be our l'chaim for this section of Hasidic translations.

There are two worlds: the lower one, which needs to be raised up to the Holy One, and the hidden world. Thus Jacob was the perfect man, dwelling in [the two] tents, raising the lower one to Him, Blessed be He.

Thus as he passes through this world, and in it finds a vital connection to God, he then can also find that connection in the hidden world. But as long as one has not yet passed through this world and found the connection in it, he cannot find the connection with God in the higher world.

So, "I have revealed my Self to Abraham, Isaac, and Jacob as El Shaddai"—the God of "enough." For God did not wish to make this world infinite so that man would be enabled to make contact with Him in the finite realm; so He withdrew to the Infinite realm. Thus, "The soul of Shaddai will give [man] understanding." That is to say that the soul will understand that it too needs to return to the infinite realm.

In this world, there is only one Shaddai-Breast [Shaddai, literally "my breasts"]. Since there is good and evil, man must not derive energies from the breast of evil, but only from the good. And even there, he is to seek holiness in what is permitted. But in the upper world, one may derive sustenance from both breasts of reality. There we can serve also with the rigors (which carry no violence). Thus the tzadikim have no peace in this world or in the World to Come. They move from rung to rung as they drink from both breasts.

"Who will give you to me as a sister to suckle from the mother's breast"—in this world, relationships are discrete and the daughter receives from the higher world. The higher world is called sister—*achot*—pointing to connectedness. Thus "who" ("*mi*"—binah, understanding) will expand and raise us to the plane where God can be served by man's deriving energies from both breasts.

There is the water from below and the water from above.

"The lower waters weep: Why must we be separated from our heavenly source?" So they yearn. When they are raised up, they sing. The lower waters are the earthly loves. They would much rather be connected to the higher love. Their yearning is so great that when they are liberated from their attachments and can flow to their divine source, they break into choral song.

The upper waters, which are "hanging," are the Torah and mitzvot. They "hang" because they would have no connection with the body if it were not for God connecting them (through the Torah and mitzvot).

The Torah was given through Moses who was victorious over the angels. The angels demanded, "Give Thy hod [glory] (Torah) to the heavenly beings," and it was Moses, through his netzach [victory] that brought the Torah down to us. Aaron, on the other hand, raised Torah up again, bringing it up to heaven, to its root. His work was in bringing peace between people and in preparing the sanctuary for God's presence. We call the act of returning energies to God by the name "hod," glorification.

If we do not raise Torah up again to God, we cannot claim to give her glory—hod. God says, "If it were not for my pact, heaven and earth I would not have set forth." In this way, Torah cannot be kept unless we participate in the attributes of Moses (netzach) and Aaron (hod). Why does the earth, the Torah, hang on *blimah*, the no-thing? Because it needs to be lived by a person who thinks of himself as no-thing; then he is in touch with the divine *ayin*, the no-thing—and thus he is connected with God and Torah; in this way, the upper and lower waters merge.

The letters (of the *Aleph-Bet*) are like a telescope trained at God. One can see Him through the lenses of love and awe in the very letters.

The spoken word yearns always to approach its origin in the larger mind—that is "the mother-bird brooding over her fledglings." "Mother" is chokhmah and binah. Where a word is spoken and the mind warms it, there the word soars to its Source—where chokhmah gives the word its beautiful form. We speak of a begotten word, one that is not merely made-spoken. When mind is inherent, the word is of the same substance as its parents.

When a person abases himself to the lowest level, his higher consciousness departs from him. This causes him great distress—therefore let him raise himself from that low level.

"I prayed to YHVH at *that time* and said" (Deut. 3:23). The purpose of serving the blessed Creator is to attain to *kalot hanefesh*, a buoyancy of the soul [when the soul is consumed in yearning and loses itself in God]. The soul is then in touch with its lust for God, and presumably the Blessed Creator too lusts for the soul—"more than the calf seeks the cow, the cow seeks the calf to suckle it." Hence the bestower is more motivated to give the good than the recipient to take it. When those yearnings coincide, all barriers are set aside, all extraneous thoughts vanish in the fervor of mutual yearning.

How does one attain this level? By realizing that all life in him flows from the Creator. It is in the nature of things that they yearn to be connected with their source. And what else is life but being one with the Blessed Creator?

This is one meaning of the Shema—"Hear Israel, YHVH our God, YHVH is One," now as He was before creation.

And creation was for the purpose of lovemaking. As long as there was only oneness, there was no delight. But when division occurred and afterwards they were connected with one another, this brought about great delight.

So one may realize that there are two times. A good time and a bad time. The Blessed Creator is termed the good time and this world is called the bad time. The purpose of it all is to raise all the life force up so that it may be included in the good. This then is the purpose of all service. A person must know that all derives from the Blessed Creator and therefore one needs to connect it all—this causes kalot hanefesh, and all the barriers fall away. All this will now help us to understand scripture. This is what is written: "David, when he changed his mind before Abimelekh" (Psalms 34:1). This means that he changed himself before God who is both *abi,* father, and *melekh,* king, and his mind refers to the cantillation (*ta'am*) that gives direction to consciousness. Thus, when David so directed his mind, he reached kalot hanefesh so that even while involved in mundane things, he raised the bad times up to the good, and this is why he sang, "I shall bless the Lord at all times," even during the bad times, so that he might raise them to the good. And this is the meaning of "And I prayed to the Lord at that time," meaning that even at *that* time, when engrossed in mundane things, we might merit to raise ourselves up to the Lord.

KABBALISTIC FOUNDATIONS

Excerpts from *Gates of Holiness* by Reb Chaim Vital

This treatise, mentioned in the section on fundamentalist Kabbalah, is typical of the works studied by those on that path. Below are two excerpts.

Gate Four

Here, greatly condensed, are the conditions for prophecy: It has already been stated that there are dents which damage the vegetative soul and there are those that damage chayah, etc. All this must be refined. Therefore, first of all, one must do teshuvah and turn away from all trespasses or vices, never to relapse into them. Then one must carefully keep all of the 248 mitzvot that apply to our times. One must take special care to set permanent times aside for the study of Torah both day and night so that not even one day be wanting. Then you must pray with perfect intention, each of the three daily prayers, to perform the benedictions and the grace after the meal with their intentions, to honor the Sabbath in all its details, and to love one's neighbor as oneself with a perfect heart, and to read the Shema, the prayers, and to observe the mitzvot of tzitzit and tefillin. One must also be guarded to keep the 365 negative commands, especially those that bring with their transgression either the death penalty by a court of man or heaven, or excommunication, and so with any "thou-shalt-nots" even in the rabbinic minutiae. Special watchfulness is necessary against tale-bearing, slander, empty talk, and mockery, or the lewd casting about of one's eyes, of all kinds of accidental seminal emissions and all kinds of approach of menstruous women and of oaths even to swear to the truth. The keeping of the Sabbath is the most important of them all.

You must also be guarded from all vices for they defile the elemental soul. Remove yourself to the very extreme from the vice of pride and liken yourself to the very lowest threshold upon which all step. The virtue of humility must become a second nature in you so that you will neither feel joy in being honored nor pain in being defamed, so that both will be equal to you. Be guarded from anger, even if you be smitten on the cheek. There is no greater obstacle to ru'ach hakodesh than anger and fussiness. You must refrain from such, even unto the very extreme, even before members of your own household. So also must you guard yourself from melancholy. Prophecy does not rest on even the most deserving one when he is melancholic. Be glad in your portion even at such times when you are beset by suffering. As it is said, "Love the Lord thy God with your whole heart." Then study the Torah for Her sake with all your strength; intend to do this only to give pleasure to your Creator. Be extremely glad when busy with the Torah and the mitzvot, as it is said, "I rejoiced over Thy word as one who finds great treasure." By doing so, you will draw great power to flow down into all the worlds. The root of all is the "awe" before Him, be He blessed, which you must generate at every moment in yourself in order not to sin. This you can achieve by visualizing the Name before your eyes as it is written, "I set YHVH before me" [*Shiviti YHVH lenegbi*]. Intend to adhere your mind to Him, not to be separated from Him even for a moment. This is the mystery of "cleave unto Him."

Gate Five

It is well clarified that Light is in the form of Man radiating in all of the four worlds—atzilut, beriyah, yetzirah, and asiyah—to the very end of the four elements in this lowly world, which itself is conjoined with the Light which is called the Ten Sefirot. They are invested into this Light of the most high Man, which is called the "Light of the Quarry whence souls are hewn." Even the lowest souls are included there. When they descend into this world to become invested in bodies of flesh, they leave their roots cleaving to the main root from whence they are hewn. Only the branches of the roots descend by spreading downward to become invested in bodies. This can be compared to a tree whose branches are at one with the roots that nourish them. When man transgresses a *karet* transgression [that carries the punishment of being cut off], he cuts the branch from the "tree" and the "roots" and remains cut off in this world like the spirit of an animal. This is the mystery of "surely shall that soul be cut off" and this too is the mystery of "for man is a tree of the field," and this too is the mystery of why the souls of the tzadikim are twice called "Abraham, Abraham," "Jacob, Jacob," and "Moses, Moses." One use of their name is to denote the root that remains cleaving to the tree on high. This is what is called man's *mazal* [star-planet or more correctly, flow-from-fount] as the sages told us how Moshe, our Master, saw the mazal of Rabbi Akiva sitting and expounding. From there the flow of the mazal proceeds to the branch that descends and invests itself in the body.

The root is most high in the very head of the world and the emanation of the branch is very long, spreading through all the worlds with only part of it investing itself in the energy of the body. In each world through which the branch spreads, it leaves a root. Hence each soul has countless roots in different worlds, one higher than the other. Through your actions, you may merit to raise them all. Thus all the roots one has in the universe of asiyah make up one's whole soul of asiyah and the same holds true on their own levels with the roots in the other rungs.

Thus the concept of prophecy can be understood in that man (when he has purged himself of all sin and of the defilement of the yetzer hara) can, by preparing himself to adhere to a particular supernal root of his being, realize it in full.

However, even if you have become worthy of this, you need to divest your soul completely and totally from all things of matter and the senses. Then only will you be capable of adhering to and realizing the spiritual root. However, this divestment, which is written about in many books, is not a complete divestment from "doing," in which the soul leaves the body—that is sleep and what is realized in it is a dream. The presence of ru'ach hakodesh in man is in the waking state when his soul is in his body, not when it has left him. What is meant by this divestment is a complete removal of thought. In thought there resides a power of *medammeh* [association, fantasy, and illusion] which makes for conceptualization. This medammeh comes from the elemental animative soul, and must be arrested and cut off from association, from weaving thoughts and mental rehearsals of worldly cravings—as if one's soul has left their body. Only then can you turn the medammeh into the direction of one of the upper worlds, into the direction of one of the roots of your soul, and proceed from one to another until your perception attains your Supernal Source. There you will become impressed by the thought forms of the "Lights," which will form themselves according to your ability to receive them in the very same quality of apperception that you have for things of this world, which are not before your eyes. Then, think and intend to receive Light from the Ten Spheres, from that point which is tangential to your soul. There you may raise the Ten Spheres up to the Infinite so that from there an illumination will be drawn down to them—to the very lowest level. When this Light is drawn down to them, they rejoice and become more luminous from that Light, which was drawn down unto them by the root of the soul that has its hold on them—in the measure that it deserved.

Then you may lead it downward step by step so that the light will reach the intellectual Soul that is in the body. From there, it will reach the animating soul and its associative powers, where the content becomes construed in material thought forms in your association. Then you will understand them in the same manner as if you had seen them with the eye of flesh. At times, this light becomes construed in the form of an angel which addresses you where you either behold him or hear him or sense him. There, a displacement and projection occurs toward the outer periphery of the sensorium that is part of the animal soul, as is well-known. Thus you see, hear, smell, and speak with your physical senses as it is written, "The spirit of God spoke in [through] me and this word was on my tongue." For the "Light" has become materialized and it took on form through the physical senses.

At other times, your prophecy will be only with the spiritual senses through the power of medammeh alone. But all this comes only as a result of diverting the physical medammeh.

In this way prophecy can be compared to a dream in which the rational soul has left the body and ascended rung by rung and arriving there, it beholds and espies and then returns and descends and draws with itself the "Light" to the animating soul and its power of medammeh where the things become construed and take on further shape. But after the soul has left the body, this does not apply.

There are two different kinds of prophecy: (a) the prophecy of all sorts of prophets whose feat of prophecy is like a trance. For they achieve Light that flows downward to the rational soul and from there, it is drawn down to the animating soul where it becomes shaped into projections of the five inner senses and their associating power. But with such seers, their outer senses may become so overwhelmed, they fall to the ground and have no strength to contain all this Light in themselves and make it visible enough for the physical senses to perceive. This kind of prophecy is called "dream," although we do not mean actual dreams but rather a "trance"; (b) the second prophecy is a perfect prophecy in which the senses are not overwhelmed but in it, all assumes its proper shape, and this is the prophecy of the quality of Moses.

The cause of this [second kind of prophecy] is that Moses had so fully clarified and refined the substance of his body, which was so completely changed by the holiness of his actions that it had attained to the level of soul. Any defilement had passed away from it and he remained so pure and good to prove that his body was never confining the powers of his soul.

It was already explained that the soul has many roots in the worlds above depending on the level of its origin, and depending on the level from which the prophet will draw forth his prophecy. Consequently, if the root of the soul originated in a higher place, the person will need to amend all the other rootlets that are below it so that he should be able to draw down from there to influence his prophecy. Otherwise he will only be able to draw forth prophecy from a level that he has already mended. Thus you will understand why there are so many levels of prophecy, and that the number of these levels is infinite. You realize therefore that it is the desire to be raised to the higher levels that opens the channel for the influence of the thoughts to be attained, as well as the intelligence to be attained, to become united with the soul and to be drawn downward. Consequently you will realize that content is verily a Light and a substance of the spiritual that comes down to the mind and through the rational soul. This influx and very real Light is what is called "thought." When you realize it fully, you will see what this means in terms of the prayerful intentions and the good thoughts of man, and also the reality of evil thoughts, which mean cleaving onto evil with one's mind. Thus you realize prophecy is a gift, which by necessity is given to each person who is able to hold onto the end of the branch of the tree. He who is capable of shaking a branch of the tree is capable of moving the entire tree. But the only way in which the upper branches will be moved is if that man has merited to draw on himself the supernal Light, and then with his thought he is able to draw down even these supernal and sublime Lights. He who has not so merited and purified himself will not find himself capable of drawing down supernal Light, for up there he will not be reckoned with at all and these Lights will not agree to come to him and to become incorporated in his thought. Vanity is developed without purification and this is no help.

“*Patach Eliyahu*” from *Tikkunei Zohar*

The Zohar and its addenda (Tikkunei Zohar) *are the main texts for Kabbalists. This excerpt is from the introduction of* Tikkunei Zohar, *and is attributed to the Prophet Elijah.*

Elijah began saying,
Lord of the worlds
You Who are One
and not just a number
You are the highest
of the highest
Most hidden
of the undisclosed
no thought scheme
grasps You
at all.

You are He
Who pours forth
Ten *tikkunim.*
We call them
the Ten Sefirot
to lead through them
Worlds
hidden and undisclosed
and Worlds manifest and known.

In them are You hidden
from the sons of men.
You are He
Who binds them,
Who unites them.

And since You are
within them
whosoever
sunders
one from its mate
of these Ten Sefirot
to him it is accounted
as if he had
sundered You.

These Ten Sefirot
proceed in their order
one—long
one—short
and one between.

You are He
who governs them.
No one
governs You
neither below
nor above
nor at any side.
You made wraps for them
(the Ten Sefirot)
from whence blossom forth
souls
for the sons of men.

Many bodies You fashioned
for them
"bodies" they are called
when compared to the "wraps"
covering them.

They are thus called
in the following tikkun:
chesed—the "right arm"
gevurah—the "left arm"
tiferet—the "trunk"
netzach and hod—the two "thighs"
yesod—the trunk's "extremity"
sign of the covenant most holy
malkhut, the "orifice"
    —the oral Torah
    we call it—
chokhmah, the "brain"
    —it is the thought
    within—
binah, the "heart"
    —in it understands
    the very heart of
    understanding.

Concerning these two,
chokhmah and binah,
it is written,
"Mysteries hidden
are they
of YHVH God."

Keter, the highest,
for it is
the crown of majesty,

concerning it is said:
"He tells the End
from the Beginning."
It is the scalp
of the tefillin
within.
It is the name "Mah"
(of numerical value forty-five)

YUD-HEH-VAV-HEH
it is the Heaven-way of
atzilut—emanation.
The rooting place of the Tree
of Boughs and Branches.
Like water
drenching the Tree
causing it to increase
through the root's sap.

O Lord of the Worlds
You are
Origin of Origins
Cause of Causes
Who drenches
that Tree
by this flux.
And this flux
like soul to body
is the body's life.

In You
There is nothing
like image
or form
of anything
within or without.

You create
Heaven and Earth
bringing forth
of their substance
Sun, Moon,
Planets, Stars.

And on Earth,
grass and trees
a garden of Eden
flora and fauna
beasts, birds, fish,
and Man.

All this so that
what is above
may become known,
so that we may have
models
of those above and below.
Those above can become known
through those below
(and since there is no model
in creation for You)
there is no one who knows
You at all.

Outside of You
there is no One
(whole—all—complete)
among those above
and those below.
Thus are You made known
as the Origin of All
and the Master of All.

Each Sefirah,
has a known Name
by these Names,
angels are called.
(An Angel—
entity of force
directed to an aim,
an energy discharged
by its own function.)

You have no known Name
because all the Names
are filled by You.
You are the fulfillment
of them all.
When You rise up from them
all the Names remain
as bodies bereft of soul.

You are wise
yet not in wisdom known.
You are understanding
yet not in understanding known.
In You there is no place for knowledge
(to hold on to).

But Your power and strength
You make knowable to Man
as You show to him
how the world
is conducted
in Law and Mercy
For there is Righteousness and Justice
according to the deeds
of the sons of Man.

Law is gevurah
Justice—the middle column
Righteousness—the Holy Majesty
the just scales
two true supports
the righteous *hin*
(liquid measure)
is the holy Covenant.

All this portrays
how the world is conducted
but not that there is
in You
known righteousness
identical with Law
(which binds You).
Nor is there Justice in You
which is Mercy
or any other attribute at all.

Be drawn down to us
Blessed channeled
YHVH
into the world
forever
truly so truly so
Amen Amen.

Notes on Sabbath Observance

During the six days of the week, we are bidden to *do*. On the Sabbath, we are bidden to cease doing, to refrain from action. How then can we live on the Sabbath?

Many of us may be able and ready to say, "I wish to do, and I want to do, and I think I even know what to do in order to make the Sabbath a day of true rest. My problem is *how* to achieve this."

What we therefore need is a functional recipe for Sabbath action and non-action. Verbal descriptions or prescriptions alone, however, will not be sufficient to provide this recipe. A person who wants to learn to drive a car needs more than verbal instruction. Nor are they equipped to drive a car even if they understand the principles of the internal combustion engine. They must be taught the function of driving the car, not in a conceptual or verbal way, but in a nonverbal way. In the same manner, we must learn to acquire what I call the Jewish body language that goes into observing the Sabbath. This language is emotive and rich in affective imagery. It is proprioceptive and not conceptual or logical. It is ancient and anthropomorphic. It does not refer to any external object. It is a language not for reason but for our imagination as it becomes translated into muscular responses. If only we knew the vocabulary of that language!

Further compounding our challenge is the fact that most of us simply do not live deliberately enough. We use the verb "to live" in a faulty manner. When I say, "I live," I (the subject) use the word *live* in its *active* form. And yet there is so much of my living that is *determined:* I am being lived by heredity, by environment, by society, by regulations, by rules. Only when I exert a conscious effort and consciously apply this effort and hold it with intention, and only when I switch off a number of habitual and automatic responses before they can become embodied in behavior, can I say that I truly live, or that I love, or that I "sabbath." For it is the duty and privilege of every Jew to be able "to make the Sabbath," *la'assot et hashabbat*—to "sabbath the Sabbath."

This is what we must learn: to "sabbath" the Sabbath. It is not altogether impossible for us to do so because we are not called upon to do something that we never before in our lives achieved. We often access a Sabbath mode during our regular weekdays though we have not labeled it as such. To begin, let's first consider our own internal circuitry.

There are two nervous systems in man. One is the sympathetic nervous system. It concerns itself with aggression and defense; it speeds up the heartbeat; it turns subjects to objects; and a man is far more determined and far less deliberate when he finds himself in the sympathetic mode of being. If we had to live only in the sympathetic mode of being, we would burn ourselves out within a short time. We have also been given another mode, the parasympathetic mode of being. In this mode we digest, eat, sleep, and procreate. We could well compare the sympathetic mode of being to the weekday mode, and the parasympathetic mode of being to the Sabbath mode. The latter is a far slower pace; the heart beats slower, one takes a far deeper and longer breath, and all energies flow down to the center.

When we fall asleep, we are usually in the parasympathetic mode of being. Conversely, when we wish to enter into the parasympathetic mode of being, we often fall asleep. If we do not wish to fall asleep, we wrench ourselves out of the parasympathetic mode into the sympathetic mode. We look for an object to vent some aggression on in order to "wake up." The stimulus that awakens us is (alas) an alarm clock. How wrong this is.

All spiritual authors agree that the parasympathetic mode of being plays a greater part in high spiritual achievement. Hence we must condition and reinforce this mode. On the Sabbath, we must learn to awaken parasympathetically. We must feel *shabbasdig*, see shabbasdig, smell shabbasdig, hear shabbasdig, and have a total shabbasdig consciousness. How can we do this?

Let me make a few suggestions. It would make little sense to argue about these suggestions. We gain no empirical evidence by arguing. Let us rather try to verify and validate them in the laboratory of our Sabbath experience. If the process works, you can do it again. If not, you may discard it, for it may not suit your own personal body rhythm or situation, and to keep it up as part of your Sabbath repertoire may hinder you instead of help.

1. **Hurried exertion**. This is a preparation. The mind must be filled with an urgency. Soon it will be Sabbath! One works up a sweat. One does not eat a full meal at noon in order to work up hunger and not merely an appetite. To work up this pre-Sabbath sweat, according to some of our spiritual authors, is considered far more purifying than a number of fast days, because by this muscular exertion, the entire body enters into the service of God.

2. **Clean the home**, even if it is already clean, or very little is left to put into order. Bathe in honor of the Sabbath, shave or fix your hair. Before this, if you can, take a dip in the lake or in a pool.

3. **Now slow the pace down deliberately**. Hum a melody slowly. Change your clothes, choose some items that you never wear except on the Sabbath. Put some money aside for tzedakah to be deposited in a tzedakah box before the kindling of the Sabbath lights.

4. **Sit in a quiet place or outdoors *alone*, not talking**. Do teshuvah for the week. Let the week's events pass before your mind's eye. Sift the good from the bad, hold the bad up to God and ask to be forgiven. If there is anyone whom you angered during the week, seek him out, ask his forgiveness, become reconciled to God and man. Breathe deeply, recollect some more and settle down into the parasympathetic mode of consciousness. Be careful to shift your senses to the Sabbath mood with a feeling such as "oh what ecstasy, I am alive." Practice what Professor Heschel calls "radical amazement."

5. **Light the candles, study a little Torah.** If a particular historic personage intrigues you especially, invite him or her for the Sabbath to be your guest in spirit.

6. **Accept upon yourself the rule of no weekday talk**, no pleasantries, no "lines." If possible, shift to Hebrew. Franz Rosenzweig found the practice of "no weekday talk" especially helpful on the Sabbath.

7. **Come early for the Friday night service** and, prior to the service, pray for the ability to serve God in the service.

8. **In prayer, serve—participate—respond—read *out*, not *in*.** Address Him. During moments of quiet, be passive and don't force any particular meditation on the Sabbath. This forcing may work during the week, but not on the Sabbath. Allow the liturgy to speak for you; give it assent by investing energies into chanting, into reading, into silence.

9. **Intend to enter into the celebrant's kiddush**, thus giving testimony to God's Blessed creatorship. Drink the wine as a special gift from the hand of Mother Sabbath. When you seat yourself at the table, wash your hands and eat the challah after the blessing. Relish the eating as a mitzvah, a holy act, dipping the bread in salt first. Eat with little talking except things pertaining to the Sabbath, to Torah and to prayer. Sing slowly and benignly; don't shout or rage in military or choreographic fashion. During the meal, intend to be like a priest who offers the mineral, animal, and vegetable kingdoms to God. Imagine and intend that you are the offering and the table the altar. Enjoy the food by chewing it slowly, and give thanks for the sense pleasure with which God has endowed the body.

10. **Chant some of the table hymns out of the prayer book.** Then recite the *Birkhat HaMazon* (the grace after meals) slowly and gratefully. Be present in every word of the Birkhat HaMazon. Take a little silent walk with a friend.

11. **When the whole evening is over, say your going-to-bed prayers.** Once you pronounce the words "into Thy hand," do not speak again until you wake up in the morning. In your thoughts give thanks to God for the Sabbath up to now. Settle down into a

relaxed sleep, all the while being aware that you are being held up by the "Everlasting Arms."

I could have illustrated each of these points by telling you many insightful stories from Hasidic tradition. I am leaving them out on purpose. The stories will come; you yourselves will live them with God's help. After the Sabbath, compare notes and reach what is called consensual validation.

The Lentchner said, "I like the mitzvah of the Sukkah best, for it is such a holy mitzvah one can enter it even with one's boots!" When the Yehudi heard this, he remarked, "I like the mitzvah of Sabbath best, for out of the Sukkah you can walk at any time, but no one can walk out of the Sabbath."

One must be very generous with God, with Mother Sabbath, with one's soul, with one's commitment, and one's decision. It is a highly expensive process, but it is rewarding in proportion to the measure of your intentional exertion.

Sabbath Time Chart

	Friday night meal and prayers	**Sabbath morning**	**Sabbath afternoon**	**Saturday night**
Mood and setting	· Gentle, expansive · At home · Eating with much singing (3/4 time) · Great variety of food · Celebrating the body · All together · Open joy · Love talk · *Japa-Bhakti*	· Quiet, reflective, intellectual · Reviewing history · *Sub specie aeternitatis* · Teaching Torah · Stately melodies (4/4 time) · Calm, head-joy · Cholent and kugel · Contemplation · *Jnana*	· Yearning, longing · Torah-dreaming about the good life · Melody: slow and recitative · Food: meager and in the synagogue · Togetherness · Tarrying · Preparation of motivation for action · Karma	· Hopeful · Story, ballad · In group at shul or at one home to which all come · Relaxed and buoyant · The fellowship of comrades · Lila
Intentions	· Homecoming · Transformation from dog to prince · Nostalgia · The haven of the old way · Harmony in the home (candles) · Past	· Awakening to unchanging realities · God is all; He is "the soul of all that lives" · The perfect order unimpeded · Ever-Present	· Realization of what tikkun is needed · Celebration of man's inherent possibility · "None is like your people Israel, one nation on earth" · Present-Future	· Charge up weekday resources · Seek vision of Elijah and his help and advice in involvement in world
Program	· Recovering the good past · History, patriarchs · The Lord Was King	· Anchoring the essential self in unchanging transcendence · Millennium · Messiah · The Lord Is King	· Promise of possible tikkun · Seek God's will: in the present, e.g., in ecology, in technology · The Lord Will Be King	· Specific action directives to further God's kingdom on earth
The archetypal person in ascendancy	Abraham · Grace · Generosity · Hospitality · Immanence · First Temple · Thesis	Isaac · Rigor and intensity · Profundity · Ideological clarity · Second Temple · Antithesis	Jacob · Mercy, beauty · Integrity · Third Messianic Temple · Synthesis	"David, King of Israel, alive existing" · Majesty

	Friday night meal and prayers	**Sabbath morning**	**Sabbath afternoon**	**Saturday night**
Antagonists and dangers	· Idolatry · Fertility cult · Hospitality without discrimination	· Divisiveness · Baseless hatred	· None	
From the Zohar and from the writings of Rabbi Isaac Luria	· Shekhinah or feminine aspect of God · "Holy orchard" · Lower paradise · Holy wedding: union of heh, vav, and heh	· "Ancient of Days" · Eyn Sof · Transcendent aspect of God · Upper paradise · God withdrawn into His yud	· The impatient lover · Masculine aspect of God · Paradise on earth · God immanent in redemptive strivings · Vav	· Shekhinah extending sustenance for next week · Adonai
From The Star of Redemption, *Franz Rosenzweig (1887–1929)*	· Creation · "In remembrance of the act of creation"	· Revelation · "Moses rejoiced" · The Sinai-gift	· Redemption · "And the Redeemer will come to Zion" · "Jacob and his children rest thereon"	· "Into Life"
Relation	· Divine-World	· Divine-Man	· Man-World	· Integration of two triangles ▽ + △ = ✡
Meal celebrates primarily	· Israel	· Torah	· God	

Finnegan's Awakening

This essay is mentioned in the discussion of the humanistic Kabbalist. It is to be read with a liquid mind.

...Once the figure ground principle is understood, we can see why the knowledge of God is not given to man in the usual manner of his cognition. Clearly, his knowledge is always of the figure and not of the ground. To focus and direct one's mind means to seek out the figure and to depress the ground. Tillich's phrase, "God, the ground of all being," serves us well. Yet despite the fact that it implies a basic invisibility of the ground, we continue to look for God as if He were a figure, the image, the eidolon. McLuhan speaks of the environment as an invisible factor. God, as the environment in which the cosmos lives, remains invisible because He is the ground that makes the figure visible. The transcendent transcends the figure and therefore is, as ground, invisible.

The search for God in the figure is doomed. God, as Alan Watts put it, is always on the inside of the inside, while anything that becomes visible ipso facto only creates other outsides as it faces the eye and reflects light from the outside—the surface. The truly immanent is invisible because it is always deeper than the surface. Once even consciousness is seen as programming, that which inheres in the programming, the knower, cannot become known. In the figure-ground situation, another dichotomous construct is hidden: subject and object. As soon as awareness turns upon itself, it has contaminated the subject, the knower, with object aims and qualities. To want to know something turns that something into a thing, an object. The subject is the opposite of the object. By definition it knows and is not known. In the figure-ground dichotomy, the figure and the ground are objects and the subject hides itself in the search for knowledge. By being made self-conscious, it fibrillates for a very small moment between the hide and seek. This touches the life-death flip and creates great anxiety. "Now you see it, now you don't" is to be conscious of everything else but not of itself. "No human shall see Me and live" (Ex. 33:20). The experience of the man who experiences his own death, and in himself sees galaxies light up is close to the experience described in the Midrash about death. We shall quote the Midrash when we speak more of death.

We recede from the fibrillation, as soon as we can manage. Being so programmed that we cannot linger in the fibrillation, we are shocked by our own adrenalin programming to let go of the subject's self-knowledge, the death revelation. With great effort, we can recall our self-encounter, but not fully. Yet we can recall it enough for the extrapolation of some ideas on how the hide-and-seek works.

We have noticed that when we inspect the length of one dichotomous construct, we begin to note the other perpendicular constructs that are necessary for the maintenance of the first. In order to make the figure-ground construct mentally visible to us, we transpose the figure-ground dichotomy from a zero position on the subject-object continuum to a plus position on the object side. Even when we know this, we do not know it fully because by that time, the game has slipped to a conceptual structure. This is another way of maintaining the object separation from the knower so that knowledge of a thing becomes possible.

Heschel is right in invoking the conceptual-situational dichotomy. But what he seems to ignore is the fact that in doing this in the form of a book, he has only reinforced the conceptual mode. (The obverse of this is that it occurs in a book held in the reader's hand—a situation.) He is no more right, however, than Buber, who divides relationships between I-Thou and I-It. To know the I-Thou and to name it is to "itify" it. Like the fifth move in cat's cradle, the figure only undergoes a topological distortion, but does not essentially change. (Obversely, is not all topology a way of showing that essential changes are only topological rearrangements?)

What am I trying to say here? (I want to give a secret away and I know that I shall not succeed, and that I will succeed—but only by indirection.) The secret I focus on will not be told. Having become the figure, it is no longer the secret and what I really want to show is only visible from the corner of the mind's eye, and not in the center of the view that the figure occupies. I do not want to tell the manifest, I want to tell the secret, but only as it becomes the manifest can it be told.

This is what the esoteric game is all about. The hidden becomes the manifest, the esoteric becomes the exoteric so that the initiate becomes privy to the secret that is no longer a secret. And this is why even the so-called mystics, the Official Kabbalists, the Hasidim, and so on, cannot lay claim to the true arcana, because there is only one Arcanum and that is that "I am God." The Creator-creature dichotomy is all that was ever created. God is All, but much of the All is programmed to think of itself as creature. The creature is nothing but an aspect of the divine omnipotence programmed to experience itself as creature.

At the moment when the creature gets too close to the secret, a flip occurs and the Knower (the Creator) protects His anonymity (His essential need not to be named) by offering another bit of knowledge. The new dichotomy is a new red herring to keep from being unmasked. (We shall return to the question, "Why must the unmasking be delayed to infinity?") In this sense, no system can exist without assistance from other systems which are perpendicular to it. The new insight contained in a new dichotomous construct, takes on significance only in relation to other dichotomies already contained within the person. The hidden, in becoming manifest, keeps the merry-go-round going to Eyn Sof.

Eyn Sof is both a condition of freedom and a condition of necessity. Adjusting to necessity, and designing such games to hide the futility of infinite changeless existence, He embraces infinity by inventing changes—short-, medium-, and long-range games, all of which are designed to hide the infinity of necessary being. How much Maimonides wished to hide, and yet how much he gave away the Necessary Existent God. How terrible. I can, at least, commit suicide. In spite of all its tragic elements, death is still a relief, because I, Zalman Schachter, am not a necessary existent. I am a variable that thinks itself an independent one, but is itself a dependent variable. Thank God, I am not a necessary existent. But I AM is.

All of change is created, moved, and flipped in order to transfer the necessity of existence onto something else. Who is it now? The fashions change and it is now someone else. Atlas is forever, but in order to get some relief, he thinks that he is now someone else. Jesus is forever on the Cross, but to ease the burden, he thinks he is now this one, now that. He splits into six million and has six million awarenesses of crucifixion. The crucial fiction is individual consciousness. The play, the game, the program that makes for a person, moves over the field of Atlas and Jesus. This is why some people make a difference between Jesus as a Christ, and THE CHRIST. This also is why there are so many Buddhas and Avatars, and in every generation there are the seven shepherds or the thirty-six tzadikim, the *lamed-vovniks*, or the righteous who each have sixty mighty men to accompany them through life. Mount Sinai is eternally poised and will crush whoever it is poised over unless he accepts the Torah. This is how He is programmed. The Torah is the program, and the experience of the poised mountain is the program.

Who did the programming? He who is the Necessary Existent! In accepting the necessity of his existence, He is It, and has to bear it all. But then comes the flip point, the extraneous thought, the temurah, and in the quick turn, He is freed and has become only a he. No longer a necessary existent, he is expendable and variable, and has at this point forgotten that he is to enter the temurah, the flip. (The seriousness with which we all obey our programming is so terribly evident as this is being written. The Arab-Israeli War is smoldering. Everyone is looking for a flipout to save face. And what is a "face"? An imagined, programmed necessity.)

How does one save face? By flipping out from the necessity and choosing another set of better necessities that are not so difficult to bear. But what about meaning? A flipout is a death of the old face. What is better? To be mortified or to be dead? Once one is on the honor-shame continuum, shame is death. A flipout is a way of changing from one continuum to the other. You decide to play economics and life games, and you may flip out of the shame-death continuum.

Life is then a game in which the goal is life, and all the continua are given to serve it. But, in order to bring the programmed ones to their senses, more death and power has to be invoked in order to push the one who is "it" to the corner where he must flip. "If you are pushed to the end of the sky—there is no more land left on which to stand—from there I shall gather you in and from there I shall take you." God, the Redeemer, is the one who is It so that the flipout in the service of life may take place. The Messiah is always a suffering servant because he takes suffering to himself and gives another the flipout possibility.

By taking an excursus, we have managed to look at the flipout by not looking at it. If we now wish to focus again on what was said, we will find it vanishing from our sight. This is part of the cul-de-sac of logical positivism; in wishing to hold on to the medium of communication, it loses the message. The immanent flees the field of vision. Shy by necessity, it will not become a figure. The ground shifts constantly, and this is why we do not see it unless we turn it into a figure; "once the ground principle is understood, we can see …"

Conclusion

Know what is above you
An eye that sees
An ear that hears
And all your actions are written in a book
—Pirkei Avot (Ethics of the Fathers)

Some assume that their book knowledge makes them high. But in truth even the greatest should not take credit for their learning. It is written that the patriarchs kept the Torah before it was given. Their illumination was so great, as were their body purifications, and the limbs and organs of their spiritual bodies were so attuned to the Divine that they saw and heard only Torah—divine will and wisdom. In that sense, we are to understand that spiritual seekers and divine wisdom are one.

The patriarchs, then, observed the entire Torah before it was given. So, "know what is above"—before you are the holy ancestors. They had "an eye that sees" and "an ear that hears." In contrast to the natural and organic way in which they saw and heard, "your actions are all written in a book" for which you have to see with the eyes of flesh and hear with ears of flesh, and it is all so forced.

So, how can anyone whose knowledge comes from books be proud?

Afterword

BeSiyata DiShmaya
with the help of the cosmos

Over time, wisdom calcifies; grand ideas harden into complex shapes that only gesture at the intricacies of the living truths they once contained. Judaism has survived as long as it has because again and again, in the eras when our wisdom is most paralyzed, we're gifted with renewal: a leader (along with a network of resonant peers and early adopters) cracks it all open to allow *mayim chaim*, God's living truth, to gush forth again. Renewal leaders like Miriam the Prophet, Rabbi Akiva, the Baal Shem Tov, and, in modern times, Reb Zalman Schachter-Shalomi, z"l.

Every great text reveals the flavorful *aspaklaria*, or subjective perspective, of the one who channels it. In this early book, Reb Zalman has not yet fully adopted the Torah of feminism, or realized the breathtaking scope of his ultimate religious vision. But his words, steeped in wonder, uncertainty, and poetic passion, still overflow with truth that can slake the thirst of any seeker. *Drink and be intoxicated, lovers!*

Reb Zalman was a pioneer in translating ancient mystical texts into modern spiritual idioms; a revolutionary in his integration of body with mind and soul; and a stunning visionary in his willingness to weave the esoteric teachings of our people's mystical masters with wisdom gleaned from Buddhist, Hindu, Islamic, and Christian traditions—offering this nutrient-rich mélange to the world without prejudice. In all this, Reb Zalman's *gadlus*, his greatness, lay in his holy spiritual chutzpah.

In one of my favorite fragments in this text, Reb Zalman recounts the hazing of a new Kotzker student. On his first morning, the other students tell him to eat before prayer. This is the way of the Kotzkers, they insist. The newcomer hesitates: only a sinner would eat before praying. But the students tell him to ask the oldest, most venerable Hasid if this is the correct thing to do. The old Hasid affirms that it is. Humbled, the new student sits down to eat, at which point the other students grab him and start yelling: "You take the word of a human being just because the old goat has a long beard! For that you will sell your God short?"

It takes enormous spiritual chutzpah to buck the authority of old goats with long beards. Reb Zalman had it in spades. His love for the living word of God was too great for him to submit to any false authority. But his spiritual chutzpah was of the most ingenious variety: he exquisitely balanced the tension between *mesorah*, the norms of tradition, and mitzvah, the divine imperative of this moment. Successfully navigating those competing forces enabled Reb Zalman to channel the revolutionary practices of Jewish meditation, egalitarian Judaism, eco-kashrut, integral halacha, and ceremonial innovation—all of which have reshaped Judaism as we know it today.

Reb Zalman's Torah is a gift for all time, but perhaps never more so than right now. Our generation has been granted one of the greatest honors and responsibilities of any generation in human history: midwifing the world through transformation on a scale we can barely fathom. We have to overhaul our economy and our communities to avert the worst of the climate crisis, negotiate a safe and healthy relationship with artificial intelligence, and call forth a healing justice to combat the fascist movements that have profoundly altered politics around the world.

This is not a *tafkid*, a deployment, for the faint of heart. We'll face frightening dangers and crushing setbacks. The stakes are terribly high. After all, not every birth ends in new life. *Chasdei Hashem*, what a blessing it is that at this critical juncture, we have Reb Zalman's Torah for guidance. The political challenges we're facing require a resurgence of politically engaged spirituality—and *that* will require alliances across boundaries of denomination and faith. Reb Zalman's Torah is a blueprint for calling on the collective moral authority of all Earth's great religious traditions to demand justice and birth *moshiachtzeit*, a more enlightened consciousness for the world. His spiritual chutzpah inspires us to buck the regressive voices of tradition that cling desperately to a status quo that is failing us on the grandest possible scale.

Whoever you are, whether you are Jewish, Jew-ish, or not Jewish—whether you're a student, a plumber, a priestess, or all of the above—you have your own vital role to play in the sacred work of our times. Renewal is essential for your work, and it offers wisdom for the challenges you're bound to face. Like any great truth, Reb Zalman's Torah, a modern incarnation of the most ancient of wisdoms, belongs to you as much as to anyone else. His legacy is *an inheritance for all God-wrestlers, for Goddexx's loving-kindness endures forever.*

May Reb Zalman's spirit be a blessing for us. As we drink from the wellspring of the Torah that Reb Zalman tapped for all humanity, may we gain the strength to birth a world of more compassion, more justice, more truth.

Ken teheya ritzona
May it be Goddexx's will

Rav Jericho Vincent

Brooklyn, New York
December 2024; Kislev 5785

Postscript

The first time I met Reb Zalman, he was with a few other people sitting in a circle, smoking a joint. I was told later that Reb Zalman believed that marijuana was a communal plant and should be shared with at least one other person, if not more. In my opinion, Reb Zalman was the real thing; he was a *Rebbe*. Over the course of our long friendship and business relationship (I was the publisher of some of his books), I saw him in action many times, telling stories or sharing his often trickster wisdom. He turned things on their head, reshaping his insights and experiences to transform people, to pierce their souls.

One day, I was walking down the country road at the Elat Chayyim Center for Jewish Spirituality when I crossed paths with a woman who looked lost. I approached her and asked if everything was okay. She told me that she had just come out of a private meeting with Reb Zalman, who was there for a week and available to meet with people one-on-one.

"How was it?" I asked with joy and enthusiasm, imagining the transformative encounter she must have had.

"Disappointing," she said.

"Do you mind if I ask why?"

"Well, I went to him asking for help and he had nothing to tell me."

"Nothing?" I asked. "He didn't say anything?" It was hard to believe.

"Nothing useful," she replied with moist eyes.

"I don't mean to pry," I said, "but could you tell me what did happen in your private time together?"

The woman told me that she was lonely and looking for her soulmate—"my *bashert*," she said—"but he had nothing to offer. He knows so many people. I figured he could suggest a person or two or offer to make some introductions. But I went away empty-handed! He offered me nothing."

"Wait a second," I replied. "He must have offered you something."

"No," she said. "Nothing."

"It's not that I don't believe you," I replied, "but are you sure he didn't say anything? Can you remember anything he told you in response to your request?"

"Well, I told him that I've been praying for so long, telling Hashem that I am so lonely and want to meet someone."

"And?" I asked.

"And he told me something of no use. He said that I might be praying for the wrong thing. Then he gave me a suggestion: rather than focusing on how lonely I was and praying to find *my* bashert, I should turn it around. Tell the Almighty that there is a wonderful person out there somewhere who is lonely and looking for their bashert. Pray that they find *their* bashert. Pray for them!"

"What an extraordinary suggestion," I exclaimed. "He might have given you the best help possible. Promise me you'll follow Reb Zalman's advice. He may have given you the key to your quandary."

I met the same woman two years later, again at Elat Chayyim. This time she was with someone, glowing. They had recently been married. She whispered to me, "Reb Zalman was right. I was praying for the wrong thing!"

·

During another week at Elat Chayyim, Reb Zalman was a guest and led the davening on Shabbos morning. When he got to the Mourner's Kaddish, Reb Zalman, who was quite gifted musically, began chanting the Kaddish in a New Orleans funeral march style. He snapped his fingers as he sang.

That day, there was a woman in attendance who had recently lost her father and was saying the Mourner's Kaddish for him. And she told a few people after the service that she was deeply offended by what she felt was Reb Zalman's inappropriate recitation of this most serious prayer. Word got to Reb Zalman about the woman's anger, and he decided to try to smooth things over.

Reb Zalman apologized to the woman, explaining that he didn't mean to offend anyone. And then he told her a story: He recalled that during the year when he was saying Kaddish for one of his parents, he walked into a small Hasidic shul in Brooklyn. Nobody there knew him, but he was asked to lead the davening—which he did. And when he got to the repetition of the Amidah and chanted the *Kedushah* (the holiest part of the service), he chanted it to the tune of "Ave Maria"!

None of the Hasidim knew the source of the melody, but after the davening was finished, a few Hasidim went over to Reb Zalman and said they had never heard such a moving, beautiful Kedushah.

Reb Zalman, upon finishing the story, looked at the offended woman and said, "You see. Tunes are tunes. They belong to the Almighty. They are in the Universe. If the Hasidim had known where I got that tune, they would have thrown me out. Instead, they were touched by its beauty."

The whole thing flipped. You could see it in her face as her whole body smiled. Another paradigm shifted.

·

On the occasion of the 50th anniversary republication of this groundbreaking book, my mind—in the spirit of Reb Zalman—wanders over to something my rebbe, Rabbi Adin Steinsaltz, once said:

> The earliest Hasidic masters were very sensitive about the need to keep the essential message pure by transmitting it directly from soul to soul. There is an emphasis in Hasidism on direct communications with one's Rebbe or teacher. It was felt that writing only creates a barrier.

> There was something dead about a book, and quite different from the direct communication between master and disciple, or between a teacher and pupil. There was an assumption that not only are the true problems of the soul left unresolved with books, but that the very essence of the message is somehow lost…
>
> During his lifetime, when a volume of sayings of the Baal Shem Tov, the founder of the Hasidic movement, came out, he dreamed that he saw a devil walking around with a book under his arm. When the Baal Shem Tov asked him what it was, the devil replied, with a smile of satisfaction, "It is a book by you, yourself."
>
> The next day, The Ba'al Shem Tov called his disciples together and demanded to know who dared to write books in his name. When he was shown the volume of his sayings, he read it and said, "There isn't a single word here that I actually spoke."[1]

Arthur Kurzweil

Scotch Plains, New Jersey
November 2024; Cheshvan 5785

NOTE

1 Arthur Kurzweil ed., *Pebbles of Wisdom from Rabbi Adin Steinsaltz* (Jossey-Bass/Wiley, 2019).

Bibliography

Ashlag, Rabbi Yehuda. *The Kabbalah: A Study of the Ten Luminous Emanations.*

Bloch, Chaim. *The Golem.*

Buber, Martin. *The Origin and Meaning of Hasidism.*

———. *Hasidism and Modern Man.*

———. *Tales of the Hasidim: The Early Masters.*

———. *Tales of the Hasidim: The Later Masters.*

Cordovero, Moses. *The Palm Tree of Deborah.* Translated by Louis Jacobs.

Dresner, Samuel H. *The Zaddik.*

González-Wippler, Migene. *A Kabbalah for the Modern World.*

Heschel, Abraham Joshua. *A Passion for Truth.*

Jacobs, Louis. *Hasidic Prayer.*

———. *Seeker of Unity.*

Kalisch, Rev. Dr. Isidor, trans. *Sepher Yezirah.*

Krakovsky, Levi. *Kabbalah: The Light of Redemption.*

Lind, Jakov. *The Trip to Jerusalem.*

Meltzer, David, ed. *Anthology of Kabbalistic Works.*

Meyrink, Gustav. *The Golem.*

Mintz, Jerome. *In Praise of the Baal Shem Tov.*

Myer, Isaac. *Qabbalah.*

Newman, Louis I., ed. *The Hasidic Anthology.*

Ponce, Charles. *Kabbalah.*

Rabinowicz, Harry M. *The World of Hasidism.*

Samuel, Maurice. *The World of Sholom Aleichem.*

Schachter-Shalomi, Zalman. *The Encounter: A Study of Counselling in Hasidism.*

———, trans. *The Torah of the Void* and "The Seven Beggars" by Reb Nachman. Available in Hasidic-Sufi Package, published by the Lama Foundations New Mexico.

———. *The First Step*. Available in Hasidic-Sufi Package.

Schaya, Leo. *The Universal Meaning of the Kabbalah.*

Schneersohn, Rabbi Joseph I. *Lubavitcher Rabbi's Memoirs.*

Scholem, Gershom G. *Jewish Gnosticism, Merkabah Mysticism, and Talmudic Tradition.*

———. *Kabbalah.*

———. *Major Trends in Jewish Mysticism.*

———. *The Messianic Idea in Judaism and Other Essays on Jewish Spirituality.*

———. *On The Kabbalah and Its Symbolism.*

———. *Sabbatai Ṣevi.*

———. *Zohar.*

Siegel, Richard, Strassfeld, Michael, and Strassfeld, Sharon, ed.. *The Jewish Catalog.*

Sperling, Harry, and Simon, Maurice, trans. *The Zohar.*

Suares, Carlo. *The Cipher of Genesis.*

Vishniac, Roman. *Polish Jews: A Pictorial Record.*

Waite, A. E. *The Holy Kabbalah.*

Weiner, Herbert. *9 ½ Mystics.*

Wiesel, Elie. *Souls on Fire.*

Zalman, Shneur. *Likutei Amarim Tanya* [English].

Zborowski, Mark, and Elizabeth Herzog. *Life Is with People.*

Rabbi Zalman Schachter-Shalomi (1924–2014), better known as Reb Zalman, was born in Poland, raised in Vienna, and ordained as a rabbi in New York. During his colorful, countercultural life, he was considered one of the foremost authorities on Kabbalah and Hasidism, and was one of the key initiators of the American Neo-Hasidic renaissance and the Jewish Renewal movement. Professor Emeritus of the Psychology of Religion and Jewish Mysticism at Temple University, and World Wisdom Chair holder emeritus at Naropa University, Reb Zalman was a unique figure in American Judaism and world spirituality, a beloved teacher and guide to many, and the author of numerous books, including *Jewish with Feeling*, *Wrapped in a Holy Flame*, *From Age-Ing to Sage-Ing*, and *Paradigm Shift*. Reb Zalman's legacy and influence remain strong, and his vision of a progressive Jewish spiritual future has inspired generations of Jews and seekers worldwide.

Eden Pearlstein is an author, artist, and cofounder of Ayin Press. He is the author of *Nothing Is for Everyone: Poems*, and coauthor/editor of the chapbooks *In/Flux: On Influence, Inspiration, Transmission, and Transformation*; *Taste and See: A Psychedelic Pesach Companion*; and *Indwelling: An Earth-Based Sukkot Companion*. Eden holds two master's degrees from JTS in Experiential Education and Jewish Philosophy. He lives in Philadelphia with his wife and two children.

Rabbi Tirzah Firestone, PhD, is an author, Jungian psychologist, and rabbi emerita of Congregation Nevei Kodesh in Boulder, Colorado. She was ordained by Rabbi Zalman Schachter-Shalomi in 1992, an experience she describes in her spiritual memoir, *With Roots in Heaven* (Dutton, 1998). Firestone lectures internationally on Jewish mysticism, the reintegration of the feminine wisdom tradition in Judaism, and the essential work of healing intergenerational trauma. Her other publications include: *The Woman's Kabbalah* (Sounds True, 2000), *The Receiving* (Harper, 2004), and the award-winning *Wounds into Wisdom* (Monkfish, 2019). See more at www.tirzahfirestone.com.

Rabbi Shaul Magid, PhD, teaches Modern Judaism at Harvard Divinity School, is a Senior Fellow at the Center for the Study of World Religions (CSWR) at Harvard University, and serves as rabbi of the Fire Island Synagogue. He works on Jewish thought and culture from the sixteenth century to the present, focusing on the Jewish mystical and philosophical tradition. His three latest books are *Piety and Rebellion* (Academic Studies Press, 2019); *Meir Kahane* (Princeton University Press, 2021); and *The Necessity of Exile* (Ayin Press, 2023). He is an elected member of the American Academy for Jewish Research and the American Society for the Study of Religion, and lives in Thetford, Vermont.

Rav Jericho Vincent is the founding rabbi of Temple of the Stranger. They are a Wexner Fellow, a member of the ROI: Schusterman Community, a recent fellow at Atra: The Center for Rabbinic Innovation, and they currently serve as an advisor to Beit Kohenet and the Shalom Center. They hold a master's degree in Public Policy from the Harvard Kennedy School and are ordained by the Aleph Ordination Program in the lineage of Reb Zalman Schachter-Shalomi. Rav Jericho has been named to the *Jewish Week*'s 36 Under 36 and the Forward 50 for their work. They live in Brooklyn on Lenape land with their partner and children. You can find them at a Temple of the Stranger ceremony, on Substack, or at www.jerichovincent.com.

Arthur Kurzweil is a writer, teacher, and magician. He is the author of several books, including *On the Road with Rabbi Steinsaltz*, *Kabbalah for Dummies*, *The Talmud for Dummies*, *The Torah for Dummies*, *Pebbles of Wisdom from Rabbi Adin Steinsaltz*, *From Generation to Generation*, and *The Persistence of Memory*. He is the recipient of the Distinguished Humanitarian Award from the Melton Center for Jewish Studies at the Ohio State University for his unique contributions to Jewish education, as well as a Lifetime Achievement Award from the International Association of Jewish Genealogical Societies. He is also a member of the Society of American Magicians and the International Brotherhood of Magicians (Order of Merlin). He and his wife, Bobby, share seven children and thirteen grandchildren.

Ayin Press is an independent publishing house rooted in Jewish culture and emanating outward.

Both online and in print, we seek to celebrate artists and thinkers at the margins and explore the growing edges of collective consciousness through a diverse range of mediums and genres.

Ayin was founded on a deep belief in the power of culture and creativity to heal, transform, and uplift the world we share and build together. We are committed to amplifying a polyphony of voices from within and beyond the Jewish world.

For more information about our current or upcoming projects and titles, reach out to us at *info@ayinpress.org*.

To make a tax-deductible contribution to our work, visit our website at *www.ayinpress.org/donate.*

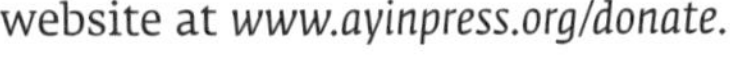